GREAT AMERICAN

FOR
JAMES BEARD
AND JULIA CHILD,
WHO LIT THE LAMP
AND SHOWED US
THE WAY

COOKING SCHOOLS

MICROWAVE COOKING
Meals in Minutes

THELMA PRESSMAN

ILLUSTRATED BY ANDREA BROOKS

IRENA CHALMERS COOKBOOKS, INC. • **NEW YORK**

IRENA CHALMERS COOKBOOKS, INC.

PUBLISHER
Irena Chalmers

Managing Editor
Jean Atcheson

Sales and Marketing Director
Diane J. Robbins

Series Design
Helene Berinsky

Cover Design
Milton Glaser
Karen Skelton, *Associate Designer*

Cover Photography
Matthew Klein

Editor for this book
Betsy Lawrence

Typesetting
Acu-Type Services, Clinton, CT

Printing
Lucas Litho., Inc., Baltimore

Editorial Office
23 East 92nd Street
New York, NY 10028
(212) 289-3105

Sales Office
P.O. Box 988
Denton, NC 27239
(800) 334-8128 or
(704) 869-4518 (NC)

LIBRARY OF CONGRESS
CATALOG CARD NO.: 83-071038
  Pressman, Thelma.
    Microwave cooking: meals in minutes
  New York, N.Y.: Chalmers, Irena Cookbooks, Inc.
84 p.

  D C B   6 5 4 3   695/16

To my beautiful family who helped me cook and cook and cook and cook and sometimes, even started without me

Contents

Acknowledgments

Since this book is about teaching, it seems appropriate to remember the teachers who have influenced me.

Dr. Bob Decareau made it possible for me, as a layman, to interact with the scientific community. A food scientist and editor, publisher of the Microwave Energy Applications Newsletter and president of the International Microwave Power Institute, he was a ray of light dispelling the misinformation about microwave cooking applications.

Ralph Wegman, my other mentor and good friend, and an electronic engineer, translated and spoon-fed back to me the enormous amount of new information coming through the scientific channels. Without Ralph's guidance the Microwave Cooking Center could not have achieved its goals or provided the quality of teaching it has been able to give.

Most of all, I acknowledge and thank my students, who demanded the best and who then became the teachers who spread the microwave word — with style. Without their constant encouragement and support the Microwave Cooking Center would never have happened.

Introduction

Microwave ovens have revolutionized the modern kitchen — and, appropriately, it all began with a candy bar. In 1946, Percy Spencer, a Raytheon scientist working with radar technology — ultra-high-frequency radio waves — noticed that a chocolate bar in his pocket had melted. His interest piqued, Spencer started to investigate the process that had caused the melting.

That process turned out to be another form of radiant energy similar to radio or light waves: microwaves, so called because they are shorter than radio waves. Microwaves are widely used in telephone relays and in short-wave and CB radio transmissions, as well as in medicine as the source of the deep-heat penetration therapy known as diathermy. Through a series of experiments it was discovered that when microwaves were confined to a box their vibrations would penetrate food and cause it to cook. It was this energy, in fact, that had melted Spencer's chocolate bar.

During the next 10 years scientists worked to develop the technology to bring microwave cooking to the home kitchen, and by 1954 the first microwave ovens were ready for the consumer market. They were large built-in units with full power broilers, used a 220-volt line and were sold for about $1,500. The early version of today's familiar countertop models reached the market in the late 1960s.

At first, not many people knew how to use them, and few recipes had been developed. But, as with most good ideas, people quickly learned, and then they shared their knowledge, so that soon cooks all over the country began learning the techniques of microwave cooking.

Improvements have kept up with the burgeoning popularity of microwave ovens, so that today the microwave oven is almost as indispensable as a dishwasher for millions of Americans. Perhaps the biggest advancement was the introduction of variable power levels in the early 1970s, which significantly increased the oven's versatility.

Most of us find it hard to give up familiar cooking methods, but every change in technology has its pioneers who charge ahead, finding excitement in new learning experiences. Without them, this book could not have been written . . . because we would probably still be cooking meat on a stick over an open fire!

How Does It Work?

Foods are cooked in a microwave oven

through the absorption of microwave power. The water molecules in the food tend to align themselves to the energy field that passes over them, making them vibrate. Microwaves actually vibrate water molecules at the rate of 2,450 million times per second, and this constant and rapid movement causes the food to heat. The top layers of the food absorb most of the microwave energy, causing the food to cook from the outside in by conduction, as in conventional cooking.

Microwave cooking has three basic principles:

1. Absorption — The moisture in food absorbs microwave energy and, the rapid movement of the water molecules heats up the food and cooks it.

2. Reflection — Metal surfaces, such as the oven wall and mesh inside the door, reflect microwave energy and do not absorb it.

3. Transmission — Glass, paper, ceramic and many plastic containers do not absorb microwave energy, thus allowing the waves to pass through to the food.

Because the microwave energy generates heat only *within* the food, the surrounding walls and utensils stay cool, leaving the interior of the oven clean. A plate of food taken directly from the oven can sometimes be quite warm, but this is only because the food on it is hot and has transmitted this heat to the plate. The microwaves themselves are not warm at all.

Know Your Oven

Microwave ovens come in a variety of makes and models. Countertop models are the most common, although combination cooking centers which include a conventional oven and range and microwave oven are also found. Microwave ovens have not yet been standardized, and the wattage of consumer models varies from 400 watts to 700 watts. The average countertop oven usually runs on 600-700 watts.

All of the recipes in this book have been developed and tested using 600-700 watt microwave ovens. If you have a 400-500 watt unit, add 30 seconds to each minute of cooking time. If your oven operates on 500-600 watts, add 15 seconds per minute of cooking time.

Microwave oven settings and cooking times vary just as they do in conventional cooking. In a conventional oven, the amount of heat entering the oven is adjusted by a thermostat. With a microwave, you adjust the frequency of vibration of the microwave energy, not the heat, because there *is* no heat except inside the food. That is what power levels are all about — simply a way of adjusting the amount of energy that is cooking the food. The higher the power level, the more cooking action.

To test your microwave power levels, place an 8-ounce cup of cold tap water in a glass measuring cup in the oven. Turn the power setting to High and set the timer for 10 minutes. Watch and record when the water comes to a rolling boil. Before repeating the test for each setting, allow the oven floor and glass cup to cool completely.

Power		Wattage Output	Time for Water Test
High	100%	600-675	2-2½ minutes
Med-Hi (⅔)	70%	400-500	3½-4 minutes
Med (½)	50%	300-350	4½-5½ minutes
Low (⅓)	30%	200-250	8½-10 minutes

Because foods differ in size, shape and moisture content, it is difficult to predict exact cooking times. In traditional cookbooks exact times are not usually given for cooking onions, for example. Instead, there will be a direction such as "cook onions until soft," leaving the cook to make the final decision. Microwave cooking is so much faster than conventional methods that the margin for error is significantly narrower and it is easy to overcook foods. This is why I have suggested more exact cooking times.

Yours is the final word, however, and the more you use your oven the more confidence you will gain. Touch or taste the food, and you will know in an instant if it is hot enough or cooked through.

Tips and Techniques

TIMING

Timing is the most important factor in microwave cooking, and it depends on many variables, including size, temperature and shape of the food, moisture content and density. Here are a few basic tips to remember:

1. The colder the food, the longer it takes to cook. Have food at room temperature to speed up cooking action.

2. Large amounts of food require longer cooking times. Energy is dispersed throughout the food rather than being concentrated on one portion.

3. Food continues to cook after the oven is turned off or the food is removed, therefore the standing time is important to finish the cooking process.

REHEATING

One of the greatest advantages of cooking in a microwave oven is its ability to reheat precooked dishes and leftovers. Quick, easy and efficient, reheating carries an extra bonus: Foods taste as though they have been freshly cooked, not tired and warmed over.

There are a few basic techniques to assure even reheating and a fresh flavor. Perhaps the most important rule, and often the hardest to remember, is *not to overheat*. One of the easiest ways to keep from overheating food is to use the sensing probe that is now supplied with most microwave ovens. The probe reads the internal temperature of the food and automatically turns the power off when it reaches a preset temperature. To use the probe, insert it horizontally into thawed food, making sure it does not touch a bone, or fat. If your oven does not have a built-in sensor probe, you can use an instant-read micro-wave-safe thermometer.

Another way to avoid overcooking is to take full advantage of the variable cooking power of your oven. Do not reheat foods at 100 percent power (High). Experiment with lower settings. On older models, use the Defrost (usually 30 or 50 percent power) or Low settings. It will take a little longer to reheat the food using lower power settings, but the results are worth the few extra seconds.

Be sure to check your owner's manual for specifics, but here are a few basic tips for reheating:

1. Bring the food to room temperature before starting to cook, if you have time. Much less energy will be required and foods will heat faster.

2. Add two or three tablespoons of water, broth or wine or a tablespoon or two of butter before reheating casseroles, vegetables and rice. Moisture and fat attract energy, reheating foods more evenly.

3. Cover foods to be reheated (see page 13).

Meat and Poultry

Reheat meat or poultry on Moderate or Low settings to keep it moist and tender. Thin slices of meat reheat more evenly and quickly than thick or irregular pieces. If you have some sauce or gravy on hand, use some of it to cover thinly sliced meats. Reheat the remainder of the sauce separately and add it at the last minute to give food an even, freshly cooked appearance.

To reheat chops, poultry parts or fillets, arrange the pieces in a round or oval shallow baking dish with the thick parts facing the sides of the dish. Use 50 percent power (Medium) to 70 percent power (Medium-High), depending on the wattage of the oven.

The temperature probe should be set at 120 degrees Fahrenheit for rare beef, lamb or veal. Bones conduct heat, so watch the meat carefully to keep it from overheating.

Main Dish Casseroles

If you are reheating a dish taken straight from the refrigerator, use 50 percent power (Medium). Room temperature casseroles can be reheated on 70 percent power (Medium-High). Microwave energy tends to concentrate around the sides of the dish, so stir through several times to promote even reheating. If you are using a temperature probe, set it at 150 or 160 degrees Fahrenheit and place it in the center of the casserole.

Soups and Stews

The temperature of reheated soups and stews is a matter of personal preference, but setting the temperature probe at 150 or 160 degrees is a good general guide. Stir through at least once while heating.

Vegetables

Sauced or creamed vegetables reheat especially well. Set the temperature probe at 150 or 160 degrees and use 50 percent power (Medium) or 70 percent power (Medium-High). Stir through several times during heating.

Cakes, Pastry, Muffins and Breads

Baked goods are the trickiest to reheat. If they are heated for even 10 seconds too long, the most tender morsel can become as hard as a rock. Bread slices, rolls and muffins take only 15 to 20 seconds each, on High, 20 to 30 seconds each if frozen. If possible, arrange them on a microwave-safe rack. Pastries with fruit fillings heat quickly because the sugar attracts microwave energy, although the crust itself may remain relatively cool.

Small Servings

One of the most convenient aspects of microwave cooking is the ability to reheat leftovers directly on dinner or serving plates, necessitating very little cleanup. For best results, follow these few hints:

1. All foods should be the same temperature.

2. Arrange the plate with thick or dense foods toward the outside rim and the more delicate foods at the center.

3. Spoon casseroles or main dishes onto plates or bowls in a shallow even layer to promote uniform heating.

4. Reheat small portions on Medium (50 percent) to Medium-High (70 percent). Food is ready when it transfers enough heat to the plate to warm it and when condensation appears under the cover.

COVERING

In general, foods that are conventionally cooked covered should also be covered in the microwave. A cover promotes steaming, leaving foods moist and tender, and helps shorten the cooking time by sealing in heat. Main-dish casseroles, fresh or frozen vegetables, poultry, meat and seafood are almost always cooked covered.

Plastic covers designed for microwave use, *casserole covers* and *plastic wrap* are the most frequently used covers, because they provide seals that assure fresh-tasting, flavorful results without dehydration. Use them for steaming vegetables that do not require added moisture. Check the package to make sure the brand of plastic wrap is recommended for microwave use.

Wax paper (or *parchment*) is an ideal covering for foods that do not require trapped steam to make them tender. It forms a loose seal that prevents spattering. Use it to make a tent when preparing poultry or seafood dishes for cooking or reheating.

Dinner plates can be used as covers for soufflé or other round cooking dishes. Saucers work well for cups or mugs, or for

small bowls. Just be sure the plates are not edged with bands of gold or silver, for the microwave action will lift off the metal.

To test your dishes to see if they are microwave-safe, put the dish in the oven next to a one-cup measure filled with water. Heat on High for 45 seconds. If the dish is hot, it is absorbing microwave energy and cannot be used. If it is only slightly warm, it is safe for reheating. If it remains cool, it can be used for extended cooking.

Cooking bags are most useful when cooking less tender cuts of meat that need moist cooking. Be sure to discard the metal twist tie, then cut a one-inch-wide strip from the open end of the bag to use as a tie. Tie loosely to allow some of the steam to escape.

Foil, contrary to popular belief, can be used in a microwave oven as long as it does not come in contact with the walls of the unit. Lightweight foil is used for shielding rather than covering. When placed over thin or cooked areas of food, it directs microwave energy toward sections that require longer cooking. Foil is also useful for defrosting, when placed over thawed sections, allowing the remaining frozen portions to continue defrosting.

White paper towel and napkins are invaluable for absorbing spatters and keeping the microwave oven clean. They do not retain heat or keep in steam, but they do absorb moisture trapped between the food and the floor of the unit. This ability to prevent sogginess makes them ideal for cooking bacon, reheating sandwiches, keeping bread surfaces dry, or as a covering for any food that contains enough moisture to be reheated without becoming dehydrated. To reheat bread or rolls, wrap them in paper towel or a napkin, elevate on a microwave-safe rack and heat on High 15 to 20 seconds per slice or roll.

BROWNING

Browning is one of the most misunderstood techniques of microwave cookery. There are many simple ways to achieve a rich brown color in foods cooked in the microwave.

Some foods brown easily in the microwave without any assistance from the cook. Small, marbleized roasts and bacon brown particularly well. When these foods are cooked on High, the fat rises to the surface and browns.

Coating large cuts of meat before cooking with chopped fresh mushrooms is an easy way to add color and flavor.

Whole turkeys and roasts must be cooked at a lower power setting to insure even cooking and tenderness. The cooking power of the lower settings is not high enough to produce browning, but commercial products, both liquid and dry, can be used to enhance the color. There are a number of dry seasoning mixes that can be used to promote browning, including some excellent products made exclusively for microwave use. But don't be afraid to experiment on your own. Dried herbs and paprika can be mixed to your taste and rubbed into meat or poultry before cooking. Dry seasonings work particularly well with skinless poultry pieces and Cornish game hens, which do not have enough fat to brown naturally during their short cooking time.

Mixes and seasonings can be applied either before or during cooking, and for a richer color can be mixed with oil, butter or drippings. When using the natural juices, cook the food about half the full amount of time, then add 1 to 2 teaspoons of browning sauce to the liquid in the baking dish and brush or baste over the food. Brush or baste the food several times during the remaining cooking time.

Popular commercial seasonings used for browning beef, poultry, lamb, fish and pork include:

Microwave shake products
Bottled browning sauce
Soy or teriyaki sauce — If desired, dilute with oil or melted unsalted butter, to your taste, to decrease the salt.
Melted butter and paprika
Worcestershire or steak sauce
Taco seasoning mix
Dry onion soup mix — Mix with dehydrated onion flakes or minced french fried onion rings, to decrease the salt.
Dry spaghetti sauce mix

Fruit preserves or jelly, or liqueurs — To enliven ham, brush on a fruit glaze after cooking; for poultry, brush on about half-way through cooking.

For other foods try:

Breadcrumbs mixed with melted butter. Use either plain toasted, herb, or Parmesan cheese varieties. Sprinkle over casseroles just after the final stirring.
Brown sugar, chopped nuts and cinnamon. Mix together and sprinkle over baked goods either during cooking or after, for a sweet brown finish.

Browning Dishes
Designed especially for microwave use, these special dishes sear and brown foods in much the same way as a skillet does, because they have a special coating that absorbs microwave energy. At maximum absorption (500-600 degrees Fahrenheit), the inside glows yellow.

Browning dishes are available in a number of sizes and shapes. Many large dishes have a well around the side to catch drippings and drain off fat. Some have ridges to give food a grilled look.

Browning dishes should always be pre-heated on High. Preheating time will vary with each recipe. The dish should absorb the maximum amount of energy before being used to cook chops and hamburgers. Once the dish is preheated, add the food to sear it and then cook according to recipe directions.

NOTE: Once food is added to the browning dish the microwave energy is attracted to the moisture in the food, not to the dish. For this reason, food can be seared on one side only unless you remove it and reheat the dish.

POACHING

Poaching is one of the easiest cooking techniques, as well as one of the most rewarding. It involves cooking food in a small amount of liquid that has been heated to just under the boiling point. Use only enough liquid to barely cover the food. This moist heat helps foods retain most of their natural juices and remain tender and flavorful. The speed and convenience of microwave cooking make it an ideal method of poaching poultry, seafood, meat, eggs and fresh fruit. Try varying the cooking liquid to heighten the flavor of the ingredients. Wine, fruit juice and broths such as fish, vegetable, meat and chicken are all good for poaching, and combinations such as chicken cooked in apple juice or seasonal fruit in wine add variety to everyday meals.

Poultry

Boned chicken or turkey breasts should be pounded to uniform thickness before cooking. Baste several times during cooking, if any portions of the meat are exposed. If the pieces vary in size, cook until almost tender and let stand, covered, in the hot liquid for several minutes.

Seafood

Use firm-fleshed fish such as rockfish, red snapper, perch, sea bass or cod; or shellfish such as scallops, shrimp or lobster.

Meat

Make sure meat is completely covered with liquid at all times. Any exposed portions will be overcooked.

Eggs

Small glass custard cups are ideal for poaching eggs. Set each cup on a saucer for easy handling, as the cups will get hot during cooking. Cover each with another saucer to trap the steam. When poaching several eggs at once, arrange the cups in a circle on a plate and cover with another plate. Gently pierce the yolks with a toothpick before cooking, to prevent bursting.

Fruit

Poach fruit in water, wine or fruit juice until just tender, then cool in the poaching liquid for at least 5 minutes before serving to heighten the flavor. Some juicy fruits can be poached in nature's own wrapping.

RECIPES

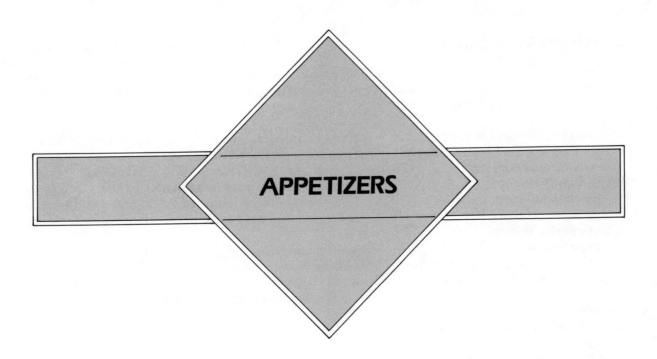

APPETIZERS

When you are making appetizers initially, select an attractive ceramic, porcelain or glass dish that will hold the heat and moisture during cooking.

Arrange chilled or frozen appetizers ahead of time on 8- or 9-inch round or oval plates rather than large platters, and let them come to room temperature before reheating. The appetizers will be nice and hot as you serve, while another batch heats in the microwave.

Try using heavy-duty paper plates to reheat appetizers and cook stuffed mushrooms for a large crowd. After heating, cover the plates with parsley, vegetables and leaves and place them on silver trays. No one will suspect that the elegant garnishes hide humble paper plates — and the cleanup will be greatly simplified.

Mexican Meatballs

These meatballs have an interesting yet mild flavor. If you prefer a hotter sauce, increase the chili powder to 1/2 teaspoon. Taste before adding — you can always add more! Serve either as an appetizer or a main dish on a bed of rice.

1 **pound lean ground beef**
1 **slice firm-textured bread, rinsed in water, squeezed dry**
1 **egg, lightly beaten**
¼ **cup chopped fresh parsley**
¼ **cup minced onion**
1 **clove garlic, minced**
1 **teaspoon salt**
⅛ **teaspoon freshly ground pepper**
4-ounce can diced green chilies

SAUCE:
1 **cup tomato puree**
¼ **cup minced onion**
¼ **teaspoon chili powder**

3 **tablespoons chopped fresh cilantro or parsley**

Combine the beef, bread, egg, parsley, onion, garlic, salt and pepper with half of the green chilies. Gently shape into small meatballs. Arrange in a circle on a round microwave-safe rack set in a shallow baking dish. Cook on High for 7 minutes. Drain off the fat, transfer the meatballs to a chafing dish or shallow serving dish and keep warm.

Combine the remaining chilies with the sauce ingredients in a large measuring cup. Cover and cook on High for 5 minutes. Spoon over the meatballs. Sprinkle with chopped cilantro or parsley and serve immediately.

Cocktail Shrimp

Both the shrimp and the tangy sauce of this elegant dish can be prepared in advance. A delicious reduced-calorie version can be made by leaving out the mayonnaise.

8 **ounces medium-size shrimp, shelled and deveined**

DIP:
3 **tablespoons mayonnaise**
3 **tablespoons bottled chili sauce**
1 **celery stalk, finely chopped**
1 **teaspoon prepared horseradish, or to taste**

Arrange the shrimp in a circle on a paper plate, tails toward the center. Cook on High for 1½ to 2 minutes, until the shrimp just turn pink; do not overcook or the shrimp will be tough. Transfer to a small bowl and let cool. Cover and refrigerate.

Combine the dip ingredients in a small bowl or container and serve with the shrimp.

Savory Chicken Wings

Makes 30 pieces

Despite their uneven shape, the chicken wings cook evenly in a round dish or pie plate. Arrange the pieces with the thicker portions facing the outside rim.

15 chicken wings
4 tablespoons butter
18 Ritz crackers
½ cup grated Parmesan cheese
2 teaspoons dried parsley
¾ teaspoon garlic powder
½ teaspoon paprika
⅛ teaspoon freshly ground pepper

Cut off the wing tips and discard. Cut the wings at the first joint. Wash and pat dry with paper towel.

Melt the butter in a 9-inch pie plate. Combine all of the remaining ingredients in a food processor or blender and mix well. Coat the chicken wings in the butter and then dip in the seasoned coating. Arrange half the wings in the pie plate, skin side up, like the spokes of a wheel.

Cover loosely with paper towel and cook on High for 15 minutes, or 1 minute per piece. Cook the remaining chicken pieces in the same way.

Mushrooms in Garlic Butter

Makes about 30

Love the sauce, but can't handle the snails? Here is my alternative.

8 tablespoons butter
3 large cloves garlic, finely chopped
1½ pounds whole small mushrooms
¾ cup finely chopped fresh parsley
¾ cup grated Parmesan cheese

Melt the butter with the garlic on High and cook until the garlic is soft, about 1½ to 2 minutes. Stir in the mushrooms and continue stirring until they are well coated. Cook on High for 3 minutes, or until slightly tender. Do not overcook. Stir and add the parsley and Parmesan cheese. Cook on High for 1 minute. Stir and serve immediately.

Mushrooms Stuffed with Cheese and Scallions

This delightful recipe won first prize from the Mushroom Growers' Association in a recent microwave cooking contest. The mushrooms can be filled ahead and refrigerated. Let them stand at room temperature for about half an hour before cooking.

**24 medium-size or large
    mushrooms
¾ cup freshly grated cheddar
    cheese
2 scallions, finely chopped
½ cup fine breadcrumbs
4 tablespoons butter, melted
½ teaspoon salt
½ teaspoon freshly ground pepper
½ teaspoon dried Italian herbs, or
    oregano
½ teaspoon Worcestershire sauce
¼ teaspoon garlic powder
Dash hot pepper sauce
Paprika, for garnish**

Remove the stems from the mushrooms and chop them finely. Transfer to a medium-sized bowl. Stir in the cheese and scallions. Add the remaining ingredients except the paprika and blend well. Fill the mushroom caps with the mixture, mounding it slightly in the center of each cap. Sprinkle with paprika. Arrange in a shallow baking dish or on a plate. Cook on High for 4 to 5 minutes, until heated through.

Liver Pâté

This pâté is good as a cracker spread or sandwich filling. The livers will cook with fewer popping sounds if you cut the membranes first. I use scissors and cut through the livers in several places. This dish requires a heavy cover during cooking, as the livers tend to move around in the casserole.

2 large onions, diced
¼ cup chicken fat, or
   4 tablespoons unsalted butter
   or salad oil
1 pound chicken livers, rinsed,
   drained and cut into pieces
1 teaspoon salt
¼ teaspoon ground white pepper
Pinch of garlic powder
1 hard-cooked egg, grated

Combine the diced onions and chicken fat or butter in a small casserole and cook on High until the onions are soft and slightly caramelized, about 10 minutes. Remove the onions from the casserole and set aside.

Place the livers in the casserole. Cover, and cook on Medium until the livers just lose their pink color, about 5 to 7 minutes; do not overcook, or the livers will be tough. Drain off any liquid and transfer the livers to a food processor. Add the onions, salt, pepper and garlic powder and process until smooth. Spoon into a bowl or other container, and chill. Garnish with the grated egg just before serving.

Polynesian Spareribs

This dish can be served as an appetizer for a large group or as a main course with a simple rice and vegetable dish and a green salad.

3 pounds pork spareribs, cut into
   sections
2 cups hot water
1 large onion, sliced
1 lemon, thinly sliced
1 cup bottled teriyaki marinade
2-3 tablespoons honey, optional

Arrange the ribs in a 3-quart baking dish, layering if necessary. Add hot water to cover. Place the onion and lemon slices on top. Cover and cook on High for 7 minutes. Reduce the power to Medium and continue cooking for 20 minutes. Turn the ribs over and rotate their position, top to bottom. Continue cooking on Medium until the ribs are tender, about 20 to 25 minutes. Drain and cut between the ribs to separate.

Combine the teriyaki marinade with the honey and dip each rib into the sauce, to coat it completely. Arrange the ribs in a spoke pattern in a shallow baking dish. Cover with the remaining sauce. Cover the dish and cook on High another 5 to 7 minutes.

Mushroom Caps Stuffed with Shrimp

Makes 24

These rich-tasting stuffed mushrooms are perfect finger food for parties. To save time stuff the mushrooms in advance and refrigerate them until party time.

8-ounce package cream cheese, at room temperature
½ pound small shrimp, cooked
2 tablespoons chopped fresh parsley
1 teaspoon garlic salt
24 large mushroom caps
6-ounce can french-fried onion rings, slightly crumbled
2 tablespoons butter

Blend together the cream cheese, shrimp, parsley and garlic salt. Stuff the mushroom caps with the mixture and scatter the onion rings over them.

Melt 1 tablespoon of butter in a 9-inch pie plate or quiche dish on High, about 1 minute. Place half of the mushrooms in the pie plate. Cook on High for 3 to 4 minutes, or until heated through. Repeat with the remaining mushrooms.

SOUPS

The great advantage of preparing soups in a microwave is that no direct heat is ever applied to the bottom of the pot, so there is less danger of burning. Although I do recommend that soups prepared in a microwave oven be stirred occasionally to insure even cooking, on the whole they require a minimum of attention. Because you do not use a metal pot, the cleanup is easy and fast.

Simple, fast soups can be made in just a few minutes and taste as though they have simmered all day. Add fresh vegetables to a can of soup to make a more substantial meal.

Soups made with raw beef and root vegetables need to be simmered on a low power setting. Begin on High to get the soup started, then reduce the power to complete the recipe.

To prepare a single serving, cook the soup in an attractive bowl, placed on a saucer.

Freeze soups in small containers or ice cube trays to provide a quick, nourishing meal or snack. Keep in mind that ice cubes do take time to defrost, even in the microwave.

San Francisco Fisherman's Soup

Serves 8 to 10

This fish soup, also known as Cioppino, takes its richly seasoned flavor from the fresh ingredients as well as the addition of a package of dry spaghetti sauce. It tastes even better when prepared a day in advance. Serve it with the Garlic Bread below.

2 cloves garlic, finely chopped
1 large onion, finely chopped
¼ cup olive oil
2 cups hot water
28-ounce can peeled plum
    tomatoes, with liquid
2 8-ounce cans tomato sauce
3-ounce package dry spaghetti
    sauce mix (preferably extra-rich
    and thick, Italian style)
¼ teaspoon freshly ground pepper
1 cup dry white wine
1½ pounds rockfish, sea bass or
    cod, cut into chunks
12 sea scallops, halved if large
8-10 large shrimp, cleaned and
    deveined, tails left on

Combine the garlic, onion and oil in a 4-quart casserole. Cover and cook on High for 4 minutes. Add the water, tomatoes, tomato sauce, sauce mix and pepper, cover and cook on High for about 10 minutes, until the mixture comes to a full boil.

Stir in the wine and add the fish, scallops and shrimp. Cover and cook on High until the fish turns opaque, about 7 to 10 minutes. Do not overcook; the fish will continue to cook for several minutes after it is removed from the oven. Let stand, covered.

GARLIC BREAD

Serves 8

This garlic bread is a little different from the usual, and my students tell me that it is their favorite. To make serving easier, you may wish to slice the bread almost through.

½ cup mayonnaise
¼ cup grated Parmesan cheese
3 cloves garlic, finely chopped, or
    1 teaspoon garlic powder
Long loaf of French or sourdough
    bread
Paprika, for garnish

Blend together the mayonnaise, Parmesan cheese and garlic.

Slice the bread in half lengthwise. Spread the garlic mixture generously over each half of the bread. Sprinkle lightly with paprika. Place each half of the loaf on paper towel on a rack to elevate. Heat on High 1 to 2 minutes, until heated through. Press down into the bread to test, keeping in mind that it will be hotter just under the surface of the bread. Avoid overheating or the bread will become tough.

Cream of Spinach Soup

I find this soup is a favorite with each new group of my students, for it is attractive, nutritious and inexpensive.

**10-ounce package frozen chopped
  spinach, thawed***
3 tablespoons all-purpose flour
1 thin slice onion
1½ cups milk
1 cup chicken broth
Salt and freshly ground pepper
1 scallion, chopped, for garnish

Puree the undrained spinach, flour and onion in a blender or food processor. Add the milk and chicken broth and process until smooth. Pour into a 2-quart bowl. Cover and cook on Medium until thickened, stirring once or twice, about 10 or 12 minutes. Taste and adjust the seasoning. Garnish with the scallion before serving.

*To thaw spinach, place the unopened box on a plate. Heat 3 to 4 minutes on High until the box feels hot to the touch. Set aside for about 5 minutes to complete defrosting.

Canadian Green Pea Soup

This is a splendid soup, in which the sweet carrots complement the flavors of the mushrooms and peas. Serve with crusty French bread.

¼ pound fresh mushrooms, diced
1 tablespoon butter
**2 11½-ounce cans condensed green
  pea soup, undiluted**
2 cups water
1 cup grated carrots
Salt and pepper, to taste

Combine the mushrooms and butter in a 1-quart bowl. Cook on High for 2 minutes. Stir in the remaining ingredients. Cover and cook on Medium-High, for about 10 minutes until the carrots are just tender. Stir once or twice during cooking. Taste, and add salt and pepper if necessary.

French Onion Soup

The traditional thick onion soup requires long, slow cooking of the onions before adding the broth and wine. Using a microwave oven cuts down on time, eliminates the possibility of scorching and reduces calories, because you use less butter.

4 pounds onions, thinly sliced
4 tablespoons unsalted butter
1 tablespoon vegetable oil
¼ teaspoon sugar
3 tablespoons flour
8 cups beef broth, homemade or canned
½ cup dry white wine
1½ - 2 cups freshly grated Parmesan cheese
1 cup freshly grated Swiss or Monterey Jack cheese

GARLIC TOAST:

1 long loaf French bread
Oil
1 clove garlic or 1 teaspoon garlic powder

Combine the onions, butter and oil in a 6-quart bowl or casserole. Cover and cook on High for 10 minutes. Stir in the sugar. Continue cooking on High for about 20 to 30 minutes, until the onions begin to brown slightly. Sprinkle with the flour and blend well. Cook on High for 1 minute.

Meanwhile bring the broth to a boil on the stove. Add to the onion mixture and stir in the wine. Cover and continue cooking on High for about 10 minutes, until the soup has thickened. Stir in ½ cup of the Parmesan. Sprinkle with ½ cup Swiss or Monterey Jack cheese.

Cut the bread into ½-inch-thick rounds. Brush with oil and rub with the cut clove of garlic or sprinkle with garlic powder. Place the rounds on a rack and cook on High until dried and lightly browned, 2 to 3 minutes.

There are two methods of serving the soup:

1. Place slices of garlic toast in the bowls and ladle the soup on top of them. Sprinkle with some of the remaining cheese and pass the rest separately. Place the bowls in the microwave and cook on High about 1 or 2 minutes, to melt the cheese.

2. Ladle the soup into individual bowls, a casserole or a tureen, float the toast rounds on the soup, cover with the remaining cheese and cook on High for 1 or 2 minutes, until the cheeses melt.

Mexican Chili Con Queso Soup

This mild but tasty soup is thick and attractive. If you reheat it, be sure to use Medium, in order to keep the cheese soft.

3 tablespoons butter
1 large onion, finely chopped
28-ounce can peeled tomatoes, chopped, with juice
4-ounce can diced green chilies
4-ounce jar pimientos, diced
Salt and freshly ground pepper
½ pound cheddar cheese, shredded
¼ pound Monterey Jack cheese, shredded
Cilantro, for garnish

Combine the butter and onion in a 3-quart casserole or soup tureen. Cover and cook on High for 7 minutes, stirring once. Stir in the tomatoes and their juice, the chilies, pimientos and salt and pepper to taste. Cover and cook on High 9-10 minutes, until the mixture comes to a full boil. Stir in the cheeses and continue cooking on High just until the cheeses melt, about 1 minute. Ladle into bowls and float a sprig of cilantro in each bowl.

Japanese Cauliflower Soup

This is a light and pretty soup which can be made with any fresh vegetable in season.

3 tablespoons butter
4 tablespoons flour
⅛ teaspoon nutmeg
4 cups chicken broth, fresh, canned or instant
1 large cauliflower, broken into florets
1 egg yolk
4 tablespoons heavy cream, or milk
1 tablespoon finely chopped fresh parsley, for garnish

Melt the butter in a 3-quart casserole. Blend in the flour and nutmeg. Stir in the chicken broth, cover and bring to a boil on High, about 7 or 8 minutes.

Add the cauliflower and stir well. Cover and cook on High for about 9 to 12 minutes, until barely tender. Mix together the egg yolk and cream, and stir into the soup a little at a time. Garnish with the chopped parsley before serving.

Old-Fashioned Lentil Soup

This recipe makes a thick, rich lentil soup, flavored with sausage and herbs.

5 cups water
½ pound knockwurst, cut into
   ¼-inch-thick slices
1 cup chopped onion
¾ cup dried lentils, rinsed and
   drained
½ cup chopped celery, with leaves
1 medium-size tomato, peeled and
   sliced
2 cloves garlic, finely chopped
2 bay leaves
½ teaspoon basil
½ teaspoon salt
¼ teaspoon white pepper
Chopped fresh parsley, for garnish

Combine all of the ingredients, except the parsley, in a 4-quart bowl or soup tureen. Cover and cook on High for 15 minutes. Stir the soup, cover and continue cooking on High for another 25 minutes. Stir again, and cook uncovered on High an additional 10 minutes. Cover and set aside for 15 minutes. Garnish with the parsley before serving.

BRUNCHES AND LUNCHES

The egg is a truly basic food — versatile, simple and delicious. From classic scrambled eggs to elegant quiches, eggs are particularly well suited to the speed of microwave cooking.

Although very easy to cook, all eggs are fairly delicate and should be cooked on lower power settings, although I find that High power and frequent stirring work well for some dishes that contain other ingredients. You should always be careful when poaching eggs to pierce the membrane that covers the yolk, or it will explode when heat builds up inside it. (This is the reason why eggs should not be cooked in the shell in the microwave!)

Quiches are numbered among those uncommon dishes that combine great flavor and simple preparation with the touch of elegance required of party food. An array of different quiches, each sliced into small servings, can take the place of an hors d'oeuvres buffet.

Puffy Omelette

Serves 2

This attractive puffy omelette makes a delicious Sunday breakfast, served with sliced tomatoes and freshly made toast.

3 eggs, separated
⅓ cup mayonnaise
2 tablespoons water
2 tablespoons butter or margarine
1 cup freshly grated cheddar cheese
Fresh parsley, finely chopped, for garnish

Beat the egg whites with an electric mixer until soft peaks form. Beat the yolks separately with the mayonnaise and water. Gently fold the yolks into the whites, blending well.

Heat the butter on High in a 9-inch pie plate for about 15 seconds. Tilt the dish to coat completely. Pour the egg mixture into the dish and cook on Medium for 7 or 8 minutes, occasionally rotating the dish if the eggs begin to cook unevenly. When the eggs are set but still moist, sprinkle with the cheese. Cook on Medium until the cheese melts, about 1 minute. Gently fold the omelette in half and slide onto a serving plate. Sprinkle with the parsley and serve immediately.

Smoked Salmon and Eggs

Serves 4

Smoked salmon, also known as lox, and eggs make a terrific brunch dish, particularly when served with bagels and cream cheese.

2 tablespoons butter or margarine
1 small onion, finely chopped
2 ounces smoked salmon, diced
6 eggs
6 tablespoons milk
Fresh parsley, finely chopped, for garnish

Melt the butter in an 8-inch pie plate on High (about 20 seconds). Tilt the dish to coat completely. Sprinkle with the onion and cook, uncovered, on High for 3 minutes, until soft and beginning to crisp slightly. Add the salmon and cook for an additional minute.

Whisk together the eggs and milk. Pour over the onions and salmon and cook, uncovered, on High for about 3 to 4 minutes, stirring from the outside in every minute until just barely set. Stir again, sprinkle with parsley and serve immediately.

South-of-the-Border Eggs

This recipe, given to me by one of my Mexican students, is one of my favorites for teaching the techniques of scrambling eggs. The chilies, tomato and onion are slightly cooked before the eggs are added, just as they are in conventional cooking. The cheese is always added last, because it melts quickly. If added too soon, the cheese will overcook before the eggs are fully cooked.

3 tablespoons butter
1 large clove garlic, finely chopped
½ small onion, finely chopped
4-ounce can diced green chilies, drained
1 large firm tomato, chopped and well drained
6 eggs, beaten
6 tablespoons milk
Salt and pepper to taste
½ cup shredded sharp cheddar cheese
2 teaspoons finely chopped fresh parsley

Cook the butter, garlic and onion in an 8-inch round quiche dish or pie plate on High for 1 minute. Stir, and cook for another minute on High. Stir in the chilies and tomato and cook on High about 2 minutes, until barely soft.

Beat together the eggs and milk. Stir in the salt and pepper. Pour over the chilies and tomato. Cook for 45 seconds, then stir from the outside toward the center. Continue cooking, 3 to 4 minutes, stirring occasionally. The eggs should remain moist, since they will continue cooking for a short time after they are removed from the oven. When the eggs are just barely cooked, sprinkle the cheese and parsley over the top. Cook on High for 1 minute, or just until the cheese melts.

Italian Sausage Quiche

The Italian sausage adds a taste to this quiche that is both mildly spicy and subtle, while the evaporated milk gives the custard flavor and helps it to set.

⅔ pound sweet Italian bulk sausage
½ cup chopped onion
2 tablespoons all-purpose flour
13-ounce can evaporated milk
4 eggs
9-inch deep-dish pie shell, prebaked (see page 78)
2 cups shredded cheddar cheese
2 teaspoons finely chopped fresh parsley

Cook the sausage, uncovered, on High until crumbly, stirring once, about 4 minutes. Drain off all of the fat. Add the onion and cook on High for 1 minute. Stir in the flour and cook on High for another minute.

Heat the milk in a 1-quart measure on High for 2½ minutes. Beat the eggs in a separate bowl. Add the hot milk and beat again.

Add the cheese to the sausage mixture and toss lightly. Spoon into the pie shell. Pour in the milk-and-egg mixture. Sprinkle with parsley. Cook on Medium-High until the center is barely set, about 12 to 15 minutes. Rotate dish, if needed. Let stand for 5 to 10 minutes before serving.

Onion Quiche

This is a surprisingly sweet and very pleasing quiche. If you have a food processor, chopping takes almost no time at all. Be careful, though, not to overprocess the onions, or they will lose their texture. Cooking onions in a microwave is especially easy, because there is no need to stir them constantly to prevent scorching.

2 pounds onions, chopped
3 tablespoons butter
2 tablespoons vegetable oil
1½ tablespoons flour
1 cup sour cream
¼ cup heavy cream
2 eggs, beaten
6 tablespoons freshly grated
  Swiss cheese
1 teaspoon salt
⅛ teaspoon freshly ground white
  pepper
9-inch deep-dish pie shell,
  prebaked (see page 78)
½ teaspoon freshly grated nutmeg
1 tablespoon finely chopped fresh
  parsley, for garnish

Combine the onions, butter and oil. Cover and cook on High until golden, about 20 minutes, stirring once or twice. Stir in the flour, cover and cook on High an additional 3 minutes.

Combine the sour cream and heavy cream. Mix in the eggs, 4 tablespoons of the cheese, the salt and pepper. Add to the onions, blending well. Pour into the pie shell and sprinkle with the remaining cheese and nutmeg. Cook on Medium-High until the center is barely set, about 12 to 14 minutes, turning the dish, as needed. Let stand 5 minutes to set. Sprinkle with the parsley before serving.

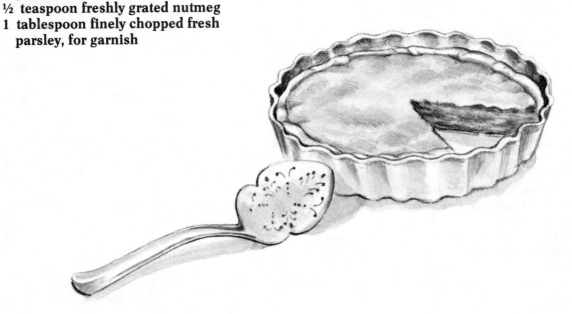

Spinach and Feta Cheese Quiche

Serves 6 to 8

The fresh color and pleasing flavors of this quiche combine to create a dish that has a slightly Middle Eastern quality.

½ cup freshly grated Parmesan
   cheese
½ cup finely chopped scallions
1 cup finely chopped fresh parsley
4 ounces feta cheese, crumbled
¼ cup fresh breadcrumbs
10-ounce package frozen chopped
   spinach, thawed and squeezed
   dry
1½ cups freshly grated Monterey
   Jack cheese
9-inch deep-dish pie shell,
   prebaked (see page 78)
1 cup heavy cream
4 eggs

Reserve 1 tablespoon each of the Parmesan cheese, chopped scallions and chopped parsley.

Combine the feta cheese with the remaining Parmesan cheese, scallions and parsley, the breadcrumbs and the spinach. Sprinkle the Monterey Jack cheese into the pie shell. Spoon the spinach mixture on top of the cheese.

Heat the cream in a measuring cup on High for 1½ minutes. Meanwhile, beat the eggs in a separate bowl. Add the hot cream to the eggs and beat again. Slowly pour the mixture over the spinach, allowing it to absorb the liquid as you pour. Sprinkle the reserved Parmesan cheese, scallion and parsley over the top. Cook on Medium-High about 12 minutes until the center is barely set, turning, if necessary, to promote even cooking. Let the quiche stand for 5 minutes before serving.

Cheese Melts

Serves 4

This dish is one of the quick snacks that a microwave oven cooks particularly well. Keep English muffins and precooked bacon in the freezer and you will always be prepared for an unexpected kitchen explorer.

2 English muffins,
   split and toasted
2 tablespoons butter, softened
4 ½-inch-thick tomato slices
8 slices crisp bacon
8 3-by-1-inch slices Swiss,
   cheddar or Monterey Jack
   cheese

Arrange the muffin halves in a baking dish or paper plate. Spread evenly with the butter. Top each with a tomato slice and crisscross with 2 slices of bacon. Overlap with 2 slices of cheese. Cook on High until the cheese melts.

Eggs with Cheese and Green Chilies *(CHILIES RELLEÑOS)*   *Serves 4*

This popular Mexican dish is increasingly seen on American tables as we realize how simple it is to prepare and how mild the chilies are when mixed with cheese and eggs. There are many versions, and I particularly like to serve this one as a Sunday brunch dish.

5 eggs
2 cups shredded Monterey Jack
   cheese
1 cup cottage cheese, well drained
¼ cup all-purpose flour
4-ounce can diced green chilies or
   ½ cup shredded green or red
   pepper, sautéed until softened
½ teaspoon baking powder

Combine all the ingredients and whisk until well blended. Pour into a 10-inch quiche dish. Cook, uncovered, on Medium-High for 12 to 15 minutes, until set. Turn the dish if it appears to be cooking unevenly.

FISH AND SEAFOOD

It is my firm belief that people who do not enjoy nature's gifts from the sea and lakes have not been fortunate enough to have this bounty properly prepared. One of the exciting things about cooking fish and seafood in a microwave is how easy it is to cook it well and preserve its moistness and natural flavor.

If you are a novice experimenting with fish, you may wish to taste as you cook, to develop a sense of timing. As in conventional cooking, the minute the fish loses its translucent appearance it is time to stop cooking. At this stage the juices are milky-looking, and the flesh is opaque. A good guide for timing is to count on about 4 minutes per pound of fish. An especially thin fillet will, of course, cook in less time.

Scallops St. Jacques

Don't let the fancy name of this classic dish frighten you. It is a delightful way to enjoy scallops.

2 large shallots, finely chopped
2 tablespoons unsalted butter
1 pound bay scallops
⅓ cup dry white wine
¼ teaspoon salt
⅛ teaspoon freshly ground white
   pepper
2 tablespoons all-purpose flour
½ cup heavy cream
1 tablespoon chopped fresh
   parsley, for garnish
Lemon wedges, for garnish

Combine the shallots and butter in a 9-inch quiche dish or pie plate. Cook on High for 1 to 2 minutes, until the shallots are soft. Stir in the scallops, wine, salt and pepper. Cook on Medium for 6 to 7 minutes, stirring once or twice. Drain the scallops well, reserving the liquid, and set aside, covered, to keep warm. Whisk a few tablespoons of the liquid into the flour to make a smooth paste. Whisk in the remainder of the liquid. Transfer the liquid to a 2-cup measure, and blend in the cream. Cook on High for 3 minutes or until thickened, without stirring, then stir through several times to blend and dissolve any lumps.

Divide the scallops evenly among individual shells or ramekins. Spoon the sauce over the scallops just before serving. Sprinkle with the chopped fresh parsley and serve with the lemon wedges.

Grilled Salmon

There is nothing quite as delicious as salmon in season, and my students tell me this is the best salmon dish they have ever tasted. You will need a browning dish to give it a grilled look.

2 salmon steaks, about 8 ounces
   each, or 1 pound salmon fillet,
   cut into 2 pieces
Vegetable oil
Freshly ground pepper
Paprika
½ lemon, sliced
Parsley sprigs, for garnish

Rinse the fish and pat it dry. Brush one side of the salmon with oil, then sprinkle with pepper and paprika. Set aside.

Preheat a medium-sized browning dish on High to maximum absorption according to the manufacturer's instructions (the timing is similar to that required for steaks and chops). As soon as it is hot, arrange the salmon in the dish, seasoned side down. Cover only if the dish has a glass lid.

Cook on High about 2 minutes, until the milky juices appear. Turn the fish over and cook an additional minute. Let it rest in the dish for a few minutes before garnishing with the lemon slices and parsley.

Rolled Stuffed Fillet of Sole with Shrimp Sauce

Serves 4

Stuffed sole covered with shrimp sauce not only tastes rich, but it looks beautiful, too. Complete the meal with a loaf of crusty French bread, a simple vegetable and rice.

STUFFING:
¼ cup thinly sliced scallions
½ cup thinly sliced celery
1 tablespoon finely chopped shallots
2 tablespoons butter
2 tablespoons finely chopped parsley
1½ cups soft breadcrumbs
¼ teaspoon tarragon leaves
¼ teaspoon salt
⅛ teaspoon white pepper

1½ pounds sole fillets
½ cup dry white wine

SHRIMP SAUCE:
3 tablespoons butter
2 tablespoons flour
¼ teaspoon salt
⅛ teaspoon white pepper
1 cup light cream or half-and-half
1 egg yolk, beaten
1 cup cooked shrimp

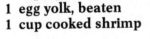

Combine the scallions, celery, shallots and butter in a 2-quart bowl. Cook on High for 3 minutes. Blend in the parsley, breadcrumbs, tarragon, salt and pepper. Cover each fillet with an equal amount of the mixture. Beginning at the thick end, roll each fillet and secure it with a toothpick. Place the fillets in a shallow round or oval baking dish. Pour the wine over the fish. Cover with wax paper and cook on High for 3 minutes. Turn the dish and cook on High for another 2 or 3 minutes. Strain and reserve the liquid.

To make the sauce, melt the butter in a 1-quart glass measure on High for 30 seconds. Stir in the flour, salt, pepper and cream. Cook for 1½ minutes on High, then stir. Add a small amount of the hot mixture to the egg yolk. Stir the yolk mixture into the remaining sauce, then add the shrimp and reserved liquid. Cook on High 1½ to 2 minutes, then stir. If you prefer a thicker sauce, continue to cook for another minute on Medium. Pour down the center of the fish and serve immediately.

Stuffed Mountain Trout

Serves 2

I always demonstrate this delicious dish as a basic cooking technique for fish. Any fish can be used, and if you like, you can use melted butter instead of wine (but the wine has fewer calories!). Use a good white wine for cooking the fish, then you can serve the remainder, pleasantly chilled, to accompany it at the table.

2 mountain trout, about 8 ounces
   each
¼ pound fresh mushrooms, sliced
¼ cup dehydrated onion
¼ cup slivered almonds
¼ cup finely chopped fresh
   parsley
¼ cup dry white wine
Salt and pepper to taste
1 lemon, thinly sliced
1 tablespoon finely chopped
   fresh parsley, for garnish

Rinse the trout and pat dry with paper towel. Combine the mushrooms, onion, almonds and parsley, and use half the mixture to fill the cavities of the fish. Place the trout in a shallow gratin dish that is just large enough to hold the fish.

Pour the wine over the trout and sprinkle with the remaining mushroom-onion-almond mixture. Overlap the lemon slices on top of each fish and garnish with chopped parsley. Cover with wax paper and cook on High for 5 to 6 minutes, just until the fish turns opaque. Be careful not to overcook.

Fish with Cheese and Caper Sauce

Serves 4

This recipe won first prize at a recent California Fisheries Association microwave cooking contest. The combination of flavors in this dish is very pleasing, and one sure to win over even those who do not normally love fish.

1 pound fresh fish fillets, such as cod, halibut, sole, or turbot
¼ cup apple cider
1 clove garlic, crushed
¼ cup sour cream
½ cup shredded cheddar cheese
2 tablespoons mayonnaise
1 tablespoon capers
1 teaspoon Dijon mustard
1 teaspoon horseradish

Place the fish in a shallow, oval baking dish and cover with the cider and the garlic. Cover, and cook on High for 4 minutes. Drain the liquid, combine it with the sour cream, cheddar cheese, mayonnaise, capers, mustard and horseradish and spread over the fish. Cover loosely with wax paper and cook on Medium for 4 minutes, or until heated through. Serve immediately.

Sweet and Sour Shrimp

Serves 4 to 6

This dish, traditionally cooked in a wok, adapts easily to the microwave oven. As in wok cooking, the ingredients are prepared in sequence depending on the amount of time they take to cook. Remember, shrimp are delicate and should be cooked only until they turn pink; overcooking makes them tough and rubbery.

3 tablespoons vegetable oil
1 medium-size onion, sliced
1 green pepper, cut into strips
1½ pounds fresh or frozen raw shrimp, shelled and deveined
16-ounce can pineapple chunks
3 tablespoons cornstarch
⅓ cup brown sugar, packed
¼ cup soy sauce
¼ cup vinegar
¼ teaspoon ground ginger
½ teaspoon black pepper
5-ounce can water chestnuts, drained and sliced

Combine the oil, onion and pepper in a 3-quart casserole. Cover and cook on High for 4 minutes. Stir in the shrimp. Cook on High for 1 minute. Set aside.

Drain the pineapple, reserving ½ cup of the syrup. Pour the syrup into a bowl, stir in the cornstarch, sugar, soy sauce, vinegar, ginger and pepper, and continue to stir until all are dissolved. Cook on High 4 to 5 minutes, stirring twice. Add the shrimp, water chestnuts and pineapple chunks. Cook on High 2 to 3 minutes, or until heated through.

Serve over noodles or a bed of rice.

POULTRY

In my home, where everyone seems to go in different directions, particularly around dinnertime, chicken is always a good choice. A 3-pound chicken cooks in about 20 minutes and is so adaptable to seasonings and sauces that it is easy to please all tastes. The leftovers are versatile, too, making delicious salads, sandwiches or hot dishes.

A whole chicken is especially well suited to microwave cooking because of its empty cavity. I prefer to start it breast side up and finish breast side down so that all of the juices flow into the white meat. Whether you choose this method or not, the bird should be turned over at least once during cooking to insure even cooking of the legs and wings. I do not cover the wings with foil during cooking, as most people enjoy them crispy.

Stuffed Roast Chicken

Serves 3 or 4

This old-fashioned dish made with modern technology will bring you compliments from family and guests every time you serve it.

½ cup finely chopped celery
½ cup finely chopped onion
2 tablespoons vegetable oil
1 cup finely chopped mushrooms
2 tablespoons finely chopped fresh parsley
½-1 cup chicken broth, heated
6-ounce package cornbread stuffing mix
A 3-4 pound chicken, cleaned, rinsed and patted dry
1 slice bread, preferably the heel
2 tablespoons butter
1 tablespoon bottled browning sauce or microwave shake product
Garlic powder, to taste
Freshly ground pepper, to taste

Combine the celery, onion and oil in a 2-quart glass measuring cup or bowl. Cover, and cook on High for 4 minutes. Stir in the mushrooms and parsley. Cook on High for 1 minute. Place the stuffing mix in a large bowl. Add the cooked vegetables and mix in the chicken broth a little at a time until lightly moistened.

Spoon the stuffing into the chicken cavity. Cover the opening with the slice of bread. Stuff the neck and secure with toothpicks. Put any remaining stuffing in a small dish.

Melt the butter in a measuring cup. Add the browning sauce and mix thoroughly. Place the chicken breast side up on a rack in a baking dish and brush liberally with the butter mixture. Sprinkle with the garlic powder and pepper. Drape wax paper over the chicken to prevent spattering and cook on High for 11 minutes. Turn the chicken over, baste with the drippings, and continue cooking on High an additional 12 to 14 minutes, until the juices run clear.

Cook the remaining stuffing on High for 3 to 7 minutes to heat through. The timing will depend on the amount in the dish. Remember — the longer it cooks, the crisper it will be. Carve the chicken and serve with the additional stuffing.

Poached Chicken Breast

Serves 2

This is a nice way to prepare chicken for recipes that call for it already cooked. Poached chicken is also delicious in sandwiches, salads, and on its own as a good, wholesome snack.

1 whole large chicken breast, boned, skinned and halved (about 8 ounces)
½ cup chicken broth

Arrange the chicken breast halves in a small oval dish and set aside. Put the chicken broth in a 1-cup measure. Cook on High for 1½ minutes, stir, and pour over the chicken. Cover, and cook on High for 4 or 5 minutes, until the chicken is tender.

Chicken Cordon Bleu

When I buy chicken, I always buy two small fryers, each weighing about 3 pounds, and bone the breasts myself. The whole breasts are quite large and can easily serve four people, depending on their appetites.

2 whole chicken breasts, boned
4 slices prosciutto ham
4 slices Monterey Jack cheese
1 egg, beaten

SAUCE:
1 tablespoon cornstarch
¼ cup dry white wine
8 medium-size fresh mushrooms, sliced
2 tablespoons freshly grated onion
1 cup shredded Monterey Jack cheese
3 tablespoons finely chopped fresh parsley

Pound each chicken breast, skin side down, in a plastic bag until thin. Place a slice of ham and cheese on each breast half and fold over. Fasten the sides together with toothpicks, if necessary.

Dip the breasts in the beaten egg. Place them, skin side down, in a shallow round or oval dish, leaving the center empty. Cook on High for 5 minutes. Turn the breasts over and baste with the drippings. Cook an additional 4 minutes, until just tender.

Remove the chicken from the dish and set aside, covered, to keep warm. Remove the skin, if you wish.

Dissolve the cornstarch in the wine. Stir the wine, mushrooms and onion into the drippings. Cook on High for 2 minutes, or until just thickened. Add the cheese and stir until melted. If necessary, cook a minute longer on High, just until the cheese melts, then replace the chicken. Spoon the sauce over the chicken and sprinkle with parsley.

Chicken Florentine with Sherry

Serves 4

Spinach and cheddar cheese blend together almost magically in this dish, bringing out the best in all the ingredients. It is wonderful for special occasions, but don't wait to make it until you are having guests to dinner. Use the Poached Chicken Breast from page 44 — and give your family a treat.

1 small onion, chopped
4 tablespoons butter or margarine
2 10-ounce packages frozen chopped spinach, thawed and well drained
2½ cups shredded cooked chicken
10½-ounce can cream of chicken soup
1 cup shredded sharp cheddar cheese
3 tablespoons dry sherry
2 slices fresh bread, coarsely crumbled in a blender or food processor
3 tablespoons butter or margarine
Paprika
2 teaspoons finely chopped fresh parsley

Combine the onion and 1 tablespoon of the butter in a 2-quart bowl. Cook on High until the onion is tender, about 3 or 4 minutes. Add the spinach and toss lightly. Spread in a 10-inch quiche dish and place the chicken on the spinach.

Combine the soup, cheese and sherry in a 1-quart glass measure and blend well. Cook on High for 4 minutes, remove from the oven and stir to melt the cheese.

Combine the breadcrumbs and remaining butter in a small glass measure. Cook on High for 1 to 2 minutes, stirring once, until the crumbs are lightly brown. Stir through the crumbs to blend.

Pour the cheese sauce over the chicken. Sprinkle the browned crumbs and paprika over the dish and cook, uncovered, on High for 10 to 12 minutes. Sprinkle with the chopped parsley.

Chicken Marengo

A traditional and popular dish has been updated here for easy preparation. It will delight both friends and family, particularly children, who usually enjoy the "spaghetti" flavor.

3-pound chicken, cut into serving pieces
1 egg white, lightly beaten
2 cups fresh breadcrumbs
3-ounce package dry spaghetti sauce mix
15-ounce can peeled tomatoes, undrained, cut with scissors
2½ cups sliced mushrooms
1 cup dry white wine

Rinse the chicken, pat dry and dip into the beaten egg white to coat thoroughly. Blend together the breadcrumbs and sauce mix. Coat each piece of chicken heavily with the crumbs. Place the pieces, skin side up, in a deep 3-quart casserole, with the white meat at the bottom and legs and wings on top. Arrange the legs so that the drums face out. Sprinkle any remaining crumbs over the top. Cook, uncovered, on High for 15 minutes.

Add the tomatoes, mushrooms and wine to the casserole. Cover, and cook on High for 10 minutes. Check at the bone for doneness and cook 5 more minutes, if needed. Serve on a bed of plain rice or pasta to give an opportunity to enjoy all of the well-flavored sauce.

Turkey Breast with Garden Vegetables

The secret of this delicately flavored dish is to precook the vegetables and then cook the turkey on top of them, so that the turkey flavors seep into the vegetables. When serving, spoon some of the vegetables over the turkey.

3 medium-size carrots
2 celery stalks
2 small onions
1 medium-size potato
3 tablespoons finely chopped fresh parsley
2 small zucchini
2 tablespoons butter or margarine
Salt and freshly ground pepper
2-3 pounds turkey breast, on the bone
Oil
Salt and pepper to taste
Paprika, for garnish

Slice the vegetables into julienne strips. Arrange closely together in a gratin dish just large enough to accommodate the turkey breast. Sprinkle in the parsley and dot the top with the butter. Season lightly with salt and pepper. Cover and cook on High for 7 minutes to steam the vegetables. Place the turkey breast on the vegetables, brush with oil and sprinkle with salt, pepper, and paprika. Cover with wax paper and cook on Medium-High 10 minutes per pound.

Almond Parmesan Chicken

Serves 2

The golden coating of almonds and Parmesan cheese makes this dish quite glamorous. It goes well with baked potatoes, steamed fresh vegetables, or rice. Use paper towel to absorb any splatters along with any extra juices, so as to keep the nut-and-cheese coating as crisp as possible.

1 cup toasted almonds, finely
   ground
½ cup freshly grated Parmesan
   cheese
1 teaspoon paprika
⅛ teaspoon salt
⅛ teaspoon freshly ground
   pepper
2 large chicken breast halves,
   skinned, boned and patted dry
1-2 tablespoons melted butter

Combine the almonds, Parmesan, paprika, salt and pepper in a shallow bowl. Dip the chicken in the butter, turning to coat evenly. Roll each piece in the nut mixture, coating it completely. Arrange the chicken, skinned side down, in a dish just large enough to hold the pieces. Cover with paper towel and cook on High for 5 minutes. Turn the chicken over and continue cooking on High for 4 minutes.

Cornish Game Hen with Wild Rice Stuffing

Serves 1

This festive dish is perfect for holidays when a big turkey is impractical. Cornish hens benefit from fairly slow cooking, so figure 7 to 10 minutes of cooking per pound. The stuffing does not add extra cooking time. This recipe makes 1 serving; to make more, follow the same techniques, increasing the amounts. Serve with a green salad and your own freshly prepared cranberry sauce (see page 72).

¼ cup sliced almonds
1 tablespoon butter
11-ounce can mandarin oranges
6-ounce package long-grain and
   wild rice
1 Cornish game hen
1 slice bread, preferably the
   heel (optional)
1 teaspoon oil
1 teaspoon seasoned salt
¼ teaspoon paprika
Parsley sprigs, for garnish
Orange segments, for garnish

Combine the almonds and butter in a 1-cup measure. Cook on High 2½ to 3 minutes, until the almonds are crisp, stirring once. Do not overcook.

Drain and measure the liquid from the oranges, adding enough water to make 1½ cups. Pour the liquid into a 1½-quart casserole, blend in the rice and the seasoning packet. Cover and cook on High for 10 minutes. Let the rice cool for 5 minutes, covered, then stir in the drained oranges and almonds. Fill the hen cavity loosely with the mixture (if any is left over, reserve it to serve as a side dish), and cover the opening with the slice of bread, or close with toothpicks. Combine the oil and the seasoned salt and brush over the skin of the hen and sprinkle with the paprika..

Place the hen breast side up in a shallow baking dish. Cover and cook on High 7 minutes per pound. To insure

even cooking and a moist texture, turn the hen over half-way through the cooking time and baste with the pan drippings.

To serve, place the hen in the center of a dish, warm through any leftover rice and arrange it in a circle around the hen. Garnish with parsley and fresh sliced orange segments.

NOTE: If you use a frozen game hen, let it defrost slowly, preferably overnight, in the refrigerator. If you are pressed for time, defrost it in the microwave set on High for 2 minutes. Allow it to rest for 5 minutes, rinse with cold water and allow to complete defrosting at room temperature. This should take about 10 minutes.

Chicken Sukiyaki
Serves 4

This popular Japanese dish is particularly good to make for guests because it not only tastes delicious, but looks quite festive. It is also versatile, for any seasonal vegetables will work well. Arrange the chicken and vegetables attractively on a large platter to display them in the traditional way before cooking. Offer additional soy sauce at the table.

½ **cup soy sauce**
½ **cup chicken broth**
¼ **cup dry sherry**
2 **tablespoons sugar**
2 **8-ounce chicken breasts, skinned, boned and cut into ½-inch slices**
6 **small mushrooms, sliced**
1 **pound fresh spinach, stems removed**
½ **pound fresh bean sprouts**
¼ **pound fresh snow peas**
½ **cup sliced celery**
1 **medium-size onion, thinly sliced**
1 **bunch scallions, halved lengthwise and cut into 3-inch pieces**

Combine the soy sauce, chicken broth, sherry and sugar in a large measuring cup. Cook on High for 2 minutes. Combine the remaining ingredients in a 3-quart casserole and toss lightly. Pour the sauce over the chicken and vegetables. Cover and cook on High for 5 minutes, stirring once after 2½ minutes. Continue cooking for 2 or 3 minutes, until the vegetables are tender. Serve over rice.

Chicken, Vegetable and Pasta Salad

Serves 8 to 10

An attractive luncheon or dinner can be built around this dish, which keeps well when prepared a day ahead. Serve with croissants or small dinner rolls, whipped butter and freshly poached fruit with a raspberry sauce.

⅓ cup pine nuts
1 teaspoon butter
6 chicken breast halves,
  boned (about 1½ pounds total)
½ cup chicken broth
1 pound linguine, cooked
  "al dente" and drained
  thoroughly
15-ounce can garbanzo beans,
  drained
2 6-ounce jars marinated
  artichoke hearts,
  with liquid
10-ounce package frozen peas,
  thawed
½ pound fresh mushrooms, sliced
2-ounce jar pimiento-stuffed
  green olives, drained and sliced
2-ounce can pitted black olives,
  drained and sliced
1 red or green bell pepper, seeded
  and cut into thin strips
½ cup olive oil
2-3 tablespoons red wine vinegar
¼ cup finely chopped fresh
  parsley
2 teaspoons Dijon mustard
½ teaspoon curry powder
1 clove garlic, finely chopped,
  or ¼ teaspoon garlic powder
Salt and freshly ground pepper

Combine the pine nuts and butter in a 1-cup measure. Cook on High, stirring once, for 2 to 2½ minutes, until the nuts begin to brown. Cool.

Arrange the chicken skin side up around the sides of a round or oval dish. Pour the chicken broth over the chicken. Cover, and cook on High for 5 minutes, then turn the pieces over. Cook on High for another 4 to 5 minutes, until the chicken is tender when pierced with a fork. Let the chicken cool in the stock, and drain thoroughly. Discard the skin and shred the meat.

Combine the pine nuts, chicken, linguine, beans, artichoke hearts, peas, mushrooms, olives and bell pepper in a large bowl and toss to blend thoroughly. Combine the oil, vinegar, parsley, mustard, curry, garlic or garlic powder, salt and pepper in a small bowl and blend well. Pour the dressing over the salad and toss well. Refrigerate until ready to serve.

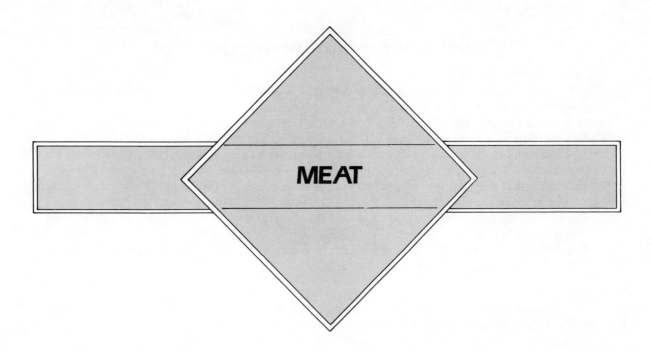

MEAT

I really enjoy cooking meat, particularly tender cuts, in the microwave because I can trim off all the fat and cut down on unnecessary calories, confident that the meat will remain tender. Cooking tender roasts is amazingly easy. If you use a sensor probe, you can turn the oven on and literally forget about the roast — no turning, no concern about timing. If I have extra time, though, I still prefer to coddle the meat by turning it over in the drippings to allow the flavors to penetrate and help it brown.

Less tender cuts of meat are treated differently. It takes long slow cooking to tenderize meats such as chuck and brisket, but long slow cooking in a microwave still takes far less time than in conventional ovens.

Most meats cook well in a microwave oven and I have included recipes here for beef in various forms from roasts to meatloaf to chops, as well as for pork and lamb.

Lamb cooks particularly well in the microwave oven. It lends itself to many variations, making it ideal for any occasion, from dinner parties to informal family suppers. Serve it roasted plain or with a sauce; in a stew or cooked in a snappy tomato-chili sauce. Braise it and combine with eggplant, basil and oregano for a Mediterranean-style dinner.

Leftover leg of lamb can be cubed and added to main-dish casseroles and spicy curries. Make sandwiches of thinly sliced lamb spread with coarse mustard, mozzarella or provolone cheese, and dark country bread. Cook on High to melt the cheese. Thin strips of cooked lamb add an elegant flavor to warm-weather main-dish salads.

MICROWAVE TECHNIQUES FOR MEAT

ROAST — TENDER CUTS

To insure even cooking, make sure frozen meat is completely defrosted before cooking, unless recipe specifies frozen meat.

Remove all visible fat.

Cook roasts in a shallow baking dish to prevent steaming.

Use a temperature probe or thermometer to prevent overcooking.

Turn roasts over at least once during cooking.

To promote a rich brown color, coat roasts with mixes, seasonings, bottled browning sauce or microwave shake product before cooking.

Cover with a white paper towel to prevent spattering. Never cover the meat with plastic wrap, or it will steam.

Let the meat stand for 20 minutes before slicing to allow the juices to settle. Place a tent of foil loosely over the roast to keep it warm.

STEWS

Use a baking dish or casserole just large enough to accommodate the ingredients. Too large a dish will allow the food to spread and cook unevenly.

Make sure the baking dish or casserole has a tight-fitting cover.

Corned Beef and Cabbage   *Serves 4*

If you have hesitated in the past to make corned beef and cabbage, thinking you didn't have the time to make it properly, wait no more. The microwave oven makes corned beef and cabbage accessible. Start the meat on High, then lower the power setting to Simmer (30 percent power), and simmer gently until tender. Add the cabbage right at the end so that it is just barely cooked.

2½-3 pounds corned beef brisket, center cut, rinsed, if desired

1 medium-size head cabbage, cut into wedges

Cut the piece of corned beef in half and place the meat in a 3- or 4-quart casserole with enough water to cover it completely. Cover and cook on High for 20 minutes. Turn the meat over and add more water, if necessary. Cover and simmer on Low (30 percent) for about 1½ hours. Let stand, covered, for 20 minutes. If it is still not tender when pierced with a fork, cover and simmer on Low an additional 10 to 15 minutes. Arrange the cabbage on top of the meat, cover and cook on High until tender, about 5 minutes. Cooling the meat in the liquid increases its tenderness. When serving, slice the beef across the grain.

Beef Tenderloin

I prefer to cook this roast without a rack so that the meat absorbs the flavors of the onions and mushrooms. Use a shallow dish, such as a medium-sized gratin dish, just deep enough to hold the meat and mushrooms snugly. The dish must be shallow or the meat will steam, not roast. If the dish is too large, the mushrooms will spread out and away from the roast. Cook on High first to facilitate browning, then reduce the power to allow the roast to cook slowly and evenly.

If your unit does not have a Roast setting, use Medium or Medium-High, 50 to 70 percent power. If your unit has only High and Defrost settings, start it on High and reduce to Defrost for the slower cooking. Be sure to let the roast stand after cooking to allow the juices to distribute evenly, for easier carving.

2-2½ pound beef tenderloin
**2-3 tablespoons dehydrated onion
  soup mix**
½ pound fresh mushrooms, sliced

Place the beef in a small shallow dish and coat evenly with the soup mix. Arrange the mushrooms over and around the roast. Place paper towel loosely over the top to prevent spattering, and cook on High for 5 minutes. Turn the meat, and spoon the mushrooms and any drippings over the top. If available, insert a microwave sensor probe into the thickest part of the roast. Cook on High an additional 5 minutes. Reduce the power level to Roast (70 percent) and cook 5 more minutes, or until the probe registers 120 degrees for rare, 130 degrees for medium-rare. Let stand 5 to 10 minutes. The internal temperature will increase about 10 degrees as it stands.

NOTE: Additional cooking time will be needed if you use a thicker butt end of fillet.

Enchilada Casserole

This tasty Mexican-style dish is very popular in our California classes, because it is mild enough to suit everyone, even children.

1½ pounds lean ground chuck
1 onion, chopped
1 clove garlic, finely chopped
1 package enchilada mix, or
    1 tablespoon chili powder
15-ounce can tomato puree
6 corn tortillas
2½ cups shredded cheddar cheese

Crumble the ground beef into a 2-quart casserole and add the onion and garlic. Cook, uncovered, on High for 3 minutes. Stir the meat, to keep it crumbly, and cook 2 minutes longer. Drain off any fat. Stir in the taco mix or chili powder and the tomato puree and cook on High for 3½ minutes.

Alternate layers of tortillas, meat sauce and cheese in a 2-quart round casserole, reserving ½ cup of the cheese. Cover, and cook approximately 7 to 8 minutes on High. Sprinkle with the reserved cheese. To serve, cut into wedges and remove each section from the casserole with a pie server.

Sausage-Stuffed Flank Steak

This dish is a good marriage of flavors and technique. When sliced, the steak reveals rich browned sausage enclosed in an attractive spiral shape.
    NOTE: The rolled steak creates a cooking pattern that tends to overcook the outside before the inside is done. Use foil to shield the ends, allowing the center to catch up.

1½ pounds flank steak,
    trimmed of fat and membrane
½ pound pork sausage
½ cup crushed saltine crackers
½ cup chopped tart apple
¼ cup chopped celery
1 tablespoon finely chopped
    onion
¼ teaspoon salt
¼ teaspoon paprika
⅛ teaspoon freshly ground
    pepper
1 tablespoon soy sauce
1 tablespoon dry white wine

Score both sides of the steak and set aside.

Place the sausage in a 1-quart measure. Cover with paper towel and cook on High for 3 minutes. Crumble the meat and drain well. Transfer to a large bowl. Blend in the crushed crackers, apple, celery, onion, salt, paprika and pepper. Spread the sausage mixture over the steak, leaving a 1-inch border on all sides. Roll up lengthwise and tie with string at each end and in the middle. Transfer the roll to a shallow baking dish. Combine the soy sauce and wine in a small cup and brush over the meat.

Cover each end of the meat with a 1-inch wide strip of foil. Cover the dish loosely with plastic wrap. Cook on Medium for 15 minutes; after 10 minutes, turn the meat over and baste it with the sauce. Discard the foil and plastic and continue cooking on Medium for 5 minutes. Let the meat stand for 5 minutes before slicing.

Oriental Beef and Noodles

Serves 4

Very little fat is required for cooking in a microwave, which makes this dish, full of fresh Oriental vegetables, both low in calories and delicious.

½ pound flank steak or beef tenderloin
2 tablespoons soy sauce
1½ teaspoons cornstarch
2 tablespoons vegetable oil
2 tablespoons freshly grated ginger root
½ teaspoon sugar
2 cups hot water
6 ounces fresh or thawed frozen snow peas
1 cup shredded Chinese cabbage
1 cup fresh bean sprouts
3-ounce package instant Oriental-style noodles with seasoning packet

Slice the steak in half lengthwise with a sharp knife, and then cut across the grain into slices about ¼ inch thick. (Partially freezing the meat will make it easier to slice.) Combine the soy sauce and cornstarch in an 11-inch oval baking or gratin dish and stir to dissolve the cornstarch. Add the oil, ginger and sugar and mix well. Stir in the beef. Leave to marinate for about 45 minutes.

Bring the water to a boil in a 2-quart bowl on High, about 6 minutes. Add the snow peas, cabbage, bean sprouts and noodles with seasoning and mix well. Cook on High for 3 minutes. Set aside, covered.

Cook the beef in its own dish on High, stirring once, 2 to 3 minutes, just until the meat loses its pinkness. Transfer the noodles and vegetables to a serving dish, spoon the beef over them, and serve immediately.

Traditional Meatloaf

Serves 6

Meatloaf is a versatile family favorite and it is great for leftovers. A slice enclosed in pita bread, with lettuce and tomatoes, makes a wholesome lunch.

1½ pounds lean ground beef
¾ cup ketchup
2 eggs
1 medium-size onion, chopped
1 clove garlic, finely chopped
2 slices bread, rinsed with cold
   water and squeezed dry
1 teaspoon Worcestershire sauce
½ teaspoon salt
¼ teaspoon freshly ground pepper

Blend together all the ingredients except ¼ cup of the ketchup. Arrange in a 6-cup ring mold, or use a deep casserole dish with a glass standing upright in the center to form a hollow well. Cook on High, turning the dish once, for about 10 to 12 minutes, until the meatloaf has pulled away from the edge of the mold. Pour off the juices. Invert the loaf onto a serving platter. Spoon the reserved ketchup evenly over the top and serve.

Pot Roast with Sherry and Vegetables

Serves 4

Imagine cooking an old-fashioned pot roast without having to scour a pot! The combination of the microwave oven and a nylon oven cooking bag makes cleaning up a simple task. If you have the time, try marinating the roast in the bag for about 2 hours before cooking to allow the seasonings to penetrate and flavor the meat.

½ cup dry sherry
¼ cup soy sauce
¼ cup water
3 cloves garlic, finely chopped
1 teaspoon dry mustard
1 teaspoon dried thyme, crumbled
¼ teaspoon ground ginger,
   or 1 slice fresh ginger root
⅛ teaspoon freshly ground pepper
2½-3 pounds chuck roast
4 carrots, peeled and cut in half
4 potatoes, peeled
3 tablespoons flour
1 large onion, sliced into rings

Cut a 1-inch strip off the open end of a 14-by-20-inch cooking bag.

Combine the sherry, soy sauce, water, garlic, mustard, thyme, ginger and pepper and blend well. Trim the meat of its fat and cut into large serving pieces. Place the meat and vegetables in the bag and sprinkle with the flour. Add the sherry mixture and the onion rings. Tie the end of the bag loosely with the reserved strip to allow steam to escape. Turn the bag gently several times to coat the meat.

Place the bag in baking dish. Cook on Simmer, or Low (30 percent), until the meat is tender when pierced with a fork, about 75 minutes. Turn the bag carefully several times during cooking. Leave the meat in the bag for 15 minutes before serving.

Zucchini Lasagna

Serves 4 to 6 as a main course, 8 to 10 as a side dish

This recipe is the brainstorm of one of my students whose garden yielded the usual bumper crops of zucchini squash. The zucchini takes the place of lasagna noodles. Make sure to drain the cooked squash completely, to avoid a watery sauce.

1½ pounds zucchini, cut lengthwise into 1½-inch-thick strips
¼ cup water
1 pound lean ground beef
¼ cup finely chopped onion
16-ounce can tomato puree
1 teaspoon garlic salt, or 1 clove garlic, finely chopped, and 1 teaspoon salt
1 teaspoon garlic powder, or 2 cloves garlic, finely chopped
1 teaspoon oregano
⅛ teaspoon freshly ground pepper
12 ounces ricotta or dry cottage cheese
½ cup freshly grated Romano or Parmesan cheese
1 egg
2 tablespoons flour
4 ounces mozzarella cheese, sliced

Place the zucchini in a 1½-quart baking dish. Add water, cover and cook on High until just tender, about 6 to 7 minutes. Drain well in a colander.

Combine the beef and onion in a 1½-quart dish or bowl. Cook on High for 3 minutes. Stir to break up the meat. Continue cooking on High until the meat is no longer pink, 1 to 2 minutes. Drain well. Stir in the tomato puree, garlic salt, garlic powder or chopped garlic, oregano and pepper. Cook, uncovered, on High for 5 minutes. Stir and set aside.

Combine the ricotta, ¼ cup of the Romano or Parmesan cheese and the egg, and blend well.

Arrange half of the zucchini slices in a large oval gratin dish. Sprinkle with 1 tablespoon of the flour. Layer with half of the ricotta mixture, then with meat sauce and mozzarella. Repeat. Sprinkle with the remaining cheese. Cook on High until heated through, about 8 to 10 minutes. If you use a sensor probe, it should read 150 degrees.

Serve with garlic bread (see page 26) and additional Parmesan cheese.

Leg of Lamb

Leg of lamb is particularly successful in the microwave. I find it has more flavor when served medium rare. If you are using a frozen leg of lamb, make sure it is completely defrosted before cooking.

Juice of ½ lemon
5- to 7-pound leg of lamb,
  excess fat removed
2 garlic cloves, crushed
1 tablespoon vegetable oil
1 tablespoon bottled browning
  sauce
½ teaspoon freshly ground pepper

Squeeze the lemon juice evenly over the lamb. Cut small slits in the fat (do not cut through to the meat) and fill with crushed garlic. Combine the oil and browning sauce in a small bowl and blend well. Brush over the lamb and sprinkle with pepper.

Arrange the lamb, thick side down, on a microwave-safe rack in a shallow baking dish. Cover with wax paper and cook on Medium 20 minutes per pound for rare and 11 minutes per pound for medium, turning the meat halfway through the cooking time.

After cooking, cover the lamb completely with foil and let stand 20 minutes before carving.

If you are using a temperature probe, insert it in the thickest portion of the meat without touching the bone. Cook to 145 degrees for medium rare, 160 degrees for medium to well-done roast.

Grilled Lamb Chops

If you have a browning dish, this simple technique for preparing lamb chops should please you. The preheated dish "grills" the meat perfectly, sealing in the juices and browning the outside. The lemon and garlic complement the flavor of the meat.

½ **lemon**
4 **loin lamb chops, about 2 inches thick**
Garlic powder, to taste
Freshly ground pepper, to taste

Squeeze the lemon juice over the chops, then pat dry with paper towel. Sprinkle the chops with garlic powder and pepper.

Preheat the browning dish on High to maximum absorption, according to the manufacturer's instructions. Remove from the oven and immediately arrange the chops in the corners of the dish. Cook on High for 3 minutes. Turn the chops over and cook on High for another minute. Let the meat stand in the dish for several minutes to finish cooking.

Lamb Riblets

Cooked this way, the riblets form tasty morsels within a sauce that is delicious served over a bed of piping-hot, freshly cooked rice.

2 **pounds lamb riblets, trimmed of fat**
1 **large onion, sliced**
½ **pound mushrooms, sliced**
8-ounce can tomato sauce
6-ounce can tomato paste
2 **tablespoons honey**
1-2 **tablespoons fresh lemon juice**
¼ **teaspoon freshly ground pepper**
⅛ **teaspoon chili powder**

Arrange the riblets in a 2-quart baking dish and sprinkle with the onion. Cover and cook on Medium-High for 10 minutes. Remove the riblets and drain off the fat. Add the mushrooms and blend well. Combine the remaining ingredients and pour over the meat. Cover, and cook on Medium until the ribs are tender when pierced with a fork, about 50 minutes. Uncover and continue cooking on Medium for another 5 minutes. Serve immediately.

Apricot-Glazed Holiday Ham

Raspberry liqueur gives the peach and apricot glaze for this ham a beautiful color and rich flavor.

5-pound precooked canned ham
8-ounce package fancy dried
  peaches
Whole cloves for studding
1 cup apricot preserves
6-ounce package extra-fancy
  choice dried apricots
½ cup raspberry liqueur
¼ teaspoon paprika

Place the ham fat side down in a baking dish. Spoon the juices from the can over the meat. Cook on High for 5 minutes. Turn the ham over and baste with the pan juices, then pour off the excess liquid.

Arrange the peaches in a layer underneath the ham to elevate it. Make sure the peaches are completely covered. Score the top of the ham in a diamond pattern. Place a clove at the points of each diamond. Brush the ham with the apricot preserves. Cook on Medium-High for 15 minutes, basting once or twice with the drippings. Remove, set aside and keep warm.

Place the apricots in a 1-quart measure. Combine the raspberry liqueur and the paprika and pour over the fruit, stirring to coat. Cook on High for 3 minutes.

Meanwhile, baste the ham with any pan drippings and arrange the peaches around it.

Remove the apricots from the raspberry mixture with a slotted spoon and arrange over the top of the ham. Brush the raspberry mixture over the ham and the peaches. Cook on High for 5 minutes, or until a sensor probe inserted in the thickest portion registers 120 degrees.

Scalloped Ham and Potatoes

Of the many ways to serve leftover ham, I am particularly fond of this hearty, soul-pleasing casserole made with sautéed onions, sliced potatoes and cheddar cheese.

2 **large onions, thinly sliced**
4 **tablespoons butter or margarine**
4 **medium-size potatoes**
   (about 2 pounds), peeled and
   thinly sliced
1½-2 **cups cubed cooked ham**
3 **tablespoons flour**
½ **teaspoon salt**
½ **teaspoon freshly ground pepper**
1½ **cups grated sharp cheddar**
   cheese
Paprika
1 **cup milk**

Combine the onions and 2 tablespoons of the butter in a 2-quart casserole. Cover and cook on High for 10 minutes, stirring once. Remove the onions and set aside.

Layer half of the potatoes and half of the ham in the bottom of the dish. Combine the flour, salt and pepper and sprinkle half of the mixture over the potatoes and ham, then layer alternately with half of the onion and half of the cheese. Sprinkle with paprika. Repeat the layering.

Scald the milk in a measuring cup on High, about 2 to 3 minutes. Pour over the casserole, cover and cook on High until the potatoes in the center of the dish are tender, about 15 to 20 minutes.

Homemade Spaghetti Sauce

1 **large onion, sliced**
¼ **cup sliced celery**
½ **green pepper, seeded and**
   thinly sliced
3 **cloves garlic, finely chopped**
2 **tablespoons olive oil**
½ **pound lean ground beef (chuck)**
14-**ounce can whole peeled**
   tomatoes, chopped, juice
   reserved
6-**ounce can tomato paste**
8 **medium-size mushrooms,**
   sliced
2 **tablespoons finely chopped**
   fresh parsley
1 **teaspoon finely chopped fresh**
   basil, or ½ teaspoon dried,
   crumbled

Combine the onion, celery, green pepper, garlic and oil in a 3-quart baking dish. Cover and cook on High for 5 minutes, stirring once. Add the ground beef and continue cooking for 3 minutes. Stir through several times. Blend in the tomatoes with their juice, the tomato paste, mushrooms, parsley and basil. Cover, and cook on High until the sauce is slightly thickened, stirring once, about 12 minutes.

Serve over freshly cooked spaghetti (1 pound spaghetti serves 4).

Pork Roast with Ginger

The combination of flavors in this roast is very pleasing, with a slight hint of the Orient. Make sure you choose a boneless roast, as it will cook more evenly and make carving easier.

1 **large onion, thinly sliced**
2-2½-**pound boneless pork**
  loin roast
3 **tablespoons dry white wine**
3 **tablespoons soy sauce**
1 **tablespoon brown sugar**
½ **teaspoon freshly ground pepper**
¼-**inch thick slice fresh ginger,**
  chopped
1 **tablespoon flour**

Cut a 2-inch-wide strip from the open end of a regular-size cooking bag and set aside.

Place the onion slices in the bag and arrange the roast over them. Blend together the wine, soy sauce, brown sugar, pepper and ginger and pour over the meat. Sprinkle in the flour. Tie the end of the bag loosely with the reserved strip. Place the bag in a shallow baking dish and simmer on Low for 15 minutes. Turn the bag over to baste the roast with the sauce. Insert a thermometer or sensor probe horizontally through the bag into the center of the meat and continue to cook on Low about 15 minutes, until the probe registers 160 degrees. Turn the bag again and let stand at room temperature until the probe registers 160 degrees. Turn the bag again and let stand at room temperature until the probe registers 170 degrees, about 10 minutes.

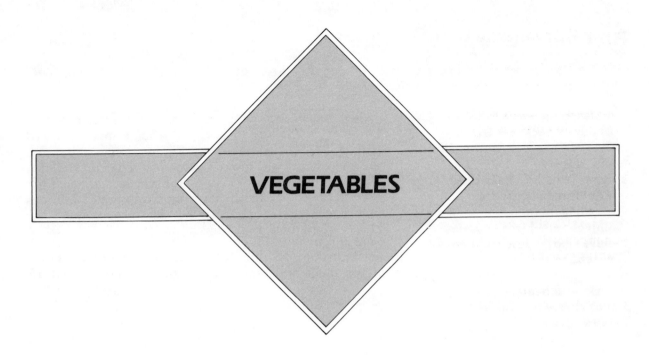

VEGETABLES

Vegetables and the microwave method were made for each other. Many vegetables taste best and retain more vitamins when they are just barely cooked, which is simple in a microwave, because the cooking process uses very little or no water. The vegetables retain their bright fresh color, and are full of flavor. If you prefer a softer texture, this, too, is easily accomplished by adding a little water and increasing the cooking time.

One of the best examples of the success of microwave-cooked vegetables is the baked potato. An oven-baked potato usually has a crisp skin and a slightly dry interior. A potato baked in a microwave retains its moisture, so that many people find they do not even desire butter or sour cream — a real bonus for dieters.

Broccoli Custard

This is a family favorite that is most easily prepared in a ring mold. The recipe can be made with almost any cooked vegetable; you will need about four cups.

2 tablespoons butter, melted
2 10-ounce packages frozen
   chopped broccoli, defrosted
   and drained
2 cups shredded sharp cheddar or
   Monterey Jack cheese
¼ cup biscuit mix
¼ cup chopped fresh parsley
2 cloves garlic, finely chopped
¼ teaspoon salt
⅛ teaspoon freshly ground pepper
4 eggs, well beaten
1 pint cherry tomatoes
Parsley sprigs

Coat the inside of the mold with the melted butter. Combine the broccoli, cheese, biscuit mix, chopped parsley, garlic, salt and pepper. Stir in the eggs and spoon the mixture into the mold. Cook, uncovered, on High for about 8 to 10 minutes, until the custard appears set around the edges. Let custard stand for about 5 minutes before turning out onto a platter. Fill the center with the cherry tomatoes and parsley sprigs. Serve warm or chilled.

Fresh Cauliflower with Cheese Sauce

This is the first recipe I adapted to microwave cooking. The cheese melts over the top to make its own sauce and combines with the tomato and breadcrumbs to make an attractive dish.

1 head cauliflower, broken into
   florets
¼ cup water
Garlic salt
Freshly ground pepper
1 large firm tomato,
   cut into wedges
¼ cup grated Parmesan cheese
¼ cup Italian seasoned
   breadcrumbs
1 cup grated Swiss cheese
1 teaspoon finely chopped fresh
   parsley, for garnish

Place the cauliflower and water in a 1-quart bowl. Cover and cook on High for about 5 minutes, until just barely tender. Pour off the water and sprinkle with the garlic salt and pepper. Arrange the tomato pieces on top of the cauliflower and sprinkle on the Parmesan cheese and breadcrumbs. Cover and cook on High for 2 minutes. Top with the Swiss cheese and cook, uncovered, on High an additional 1 to 2 minutes, just until the cheese is melted. Sprinkle with parsley and serve immediately.

Corn in the Husk

Everything peels off easily when corn is cooked this way — even the silk. By soaking the corn first, you clean off any soil and moisten the leaves, which then steam the kernels they enclose.

4 ears corn, in their husks

Remove any dry outside leaves from the corn and discard. Place the ears of corn in the sink with enough cold water to cover. Soak for 5 minutes. Transfer to a dish and cook on High for 12 minutes, or until tender. Cooking time should be about 3 minutes per ear of corn. Peel the husks from the top like a banana. You will find that the silk peels along with the husk.

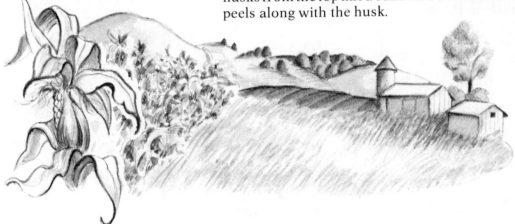

Carrot Puree on Summer Squash

If vegetables can be said to have personality, these squash with their rakish hats certainly have it. But the dish is more than merely attractive — it tastes absolutely delicious.

½ pound carrots, cut into 1-inch pieces
1 tablespoon water
1 tablespoon butter
½ teaspoon orange marmalade
Salt and freshly ground white pepper, to taste
6 medium-size pattypan squash, with stems

Combine the carrots and water in a 1-quart casserole. Cook, covered, on High for 5 to 6 minutes. Drain thoroughly. Place the carrots in a food processor or blender, add the butter and puree until smooth. Add the marmalade, salt and pepper and mix well. Set aside to cool.

Place the squash in a 1-quart casserole. Cook, covered, until tender, about 4 minutes. Let the squash cool slightly, then slice off each top to form a lid. Spoon the carrot puree over each opening and replace the squash tops at an angle. Cover lightly with wax paper and cook on Medium-High until heated through, about 2 minutes.

Western Vegetable Medley

This beautiful presentation dish is an old favorite of mine, and the recipe I developed to inaugurate my microwave cooking center in 1968. It has since become a standard for many teachers and appears in microwave cookbooks all over the world.

1 medium-size zucchini squash
1 medium-size crookneck squash
1 medium-size pattypan squash
½ small cauliflower
1 bunch broccoli
3 large fresh mushrooms
½ red pepper
½ green pepper
4 tablespoons butter
Garlic salt and seasoned pepper
   to taste

Rinse the squash and slice into rounds about ¼ inch thick. Break the cauliflower into florets, cutting them in half if thick. Cut the broccoli into florets, leaving some of the stem on each. Cut slits in the stems, if thick. Slice the mushrooms. Cut the peppers into strips.

Select a large round platter that will fill as much of the microwave as possible, about 12 inches in diameter. Place the broccoli in a circle around the outside of the platter. Arrange the cauliflower in a ring inside the broccoli. Arrange the other vegetables in the center, alternating colors.

Melt the butter and pour it over the vegetables. Season with garlic salt and pepper. Cover with plastic wrap and cook on High for 7 to 9 minutes, until the vegetables are just tender. Remember, they will continue to cook for a few minutes, so don't let them overcook — they should remain crisp.

Baked Potato

This may well become the classic baked potato. It is moist and flavorful, requiring only salt and pepper for seasoning. The potato is baked on an elevated rack so that it cooks evenly without trapping steam underneath.

A large (6- to 8-ounce) potato
Salt and pepper to taste

Wash the potato and pat it dry. Place on a microwave-safe rack and cook on High until the outside feels slightly soft, about 4 to 6 minutes. Allow it to sit and finish cooking for a few minutes before cutting.

To bake several potatoes at a time, place them in a circle on the rack. Four potatoes will take about 20 minutes. Add about 2 minutes cooking time for each additional potato. If the potatoes vary in size, remove the smaller ones as they become soft, allowing the larger ones to continue cooking.

If you prefer the traditional crisp-skinned potato, place the cooked potato in a toaster oven set at 400 degrees. Bake for 5 minutes, or until the skin is crisp.

Twice-Baked Potatoes

This recipe is for true potato lovers. Adapt it to your own taste by varying the cheese and bacon. When prepared with a mixer, it requires very little time or effort.

4 baking potatoes
8 tablespoons butter
½ cup sour cream
¼ cup shredded cheddar cheese
½ teaspoon salt
Pinch freshly ground pepper
4 teaspoons crumbled cooked
bacon (optional)
Chopped chives
Paprika

Arrange the potatoes in a circle on a microwave-safe rack, spacing them about 1 inch apart. Cook on High 12 to 14 minutes, until the potatoes begin to feel soft. Let stand for 2 to 4 minutes. Slice the top off each potato. Scoop out the pulp carefully and transfer it to a mixing bowl. Add the butter, sour cream, cheddar cheese, salt and pepper. Beat with a mixer until smooth.

Fill the potato shells with the mixture, mounding it slightly in the centers. Sprinkle each with 1 teaspoon bacon, chives and paprika. Arrange the potatoes in a circle about 1 inch apart on a serving plate. Cook on High until hot, about 4 minutes. Serve immediately.

Seasoned Rice

Rice cooked in the microwave oven really does turn out perfectly every time.

2 cups water
1 cup long-grain converted rice
¼ cup dehydrated onion
2 teaspoons chicken or beef
  bouillon crystals

Combine all the ingredients in a 3-quart casserole. Cover lightly and cook on High for 12 minutes. Let stand, covered, for 5 minutes, or until all the water is absorbed.

To reheat, add about 3 tablespoons of water for each cup of cooked rice and reheat on High for 2 minutes per cup of rice.

Potato Soufflé

When I want to impress people with something simple but delicious, I prepare this potato soufflé. I always find the combination of onions cooked in butter, mashed potatoes, sour cream, eggs and cheese deliciously rich and satisfying. If you are pressed for time, you can make this dish ahead and reheat it. Leftovers can be frozen in individual servings and reheated as needed.

8 tablespoons butter
1 pound yellow onions, thinly
  sliced
2 pounds potatoes
¾ cup milk
½ cup sour cream
1 teaspoon baking powder
2 eggs, well beaten
1 teaspoon salt
¼ teaspoon white pepper
1¼ cups freshly grated cheddar
  cheese
1 teaspoon finely chopped fresh
  parsley

Melt 4 tablespoons of the butter in a 1½-quart soufflé dish. Stir in the onion. Cover and cook on High for about 15 to 20 minutes, until the onion is lightly brown in spots. Stir several times as they cook. Remove the dish and set aside.

Arrange the unpeeled potatoes in a circle on a rack. Cook on High until just soft, about 5 or 6 minutes per potato. (If some cook faster than others, remove them and continue cooking the remainder.) Let stand 5 minutes.

Peel and quarter the potatoes and place them in a large mixing bowl. Add the remaining butter, the milk, sour cream and baking powder and whip until smooth. Add the beaten eggs, salt and pepper and continue whipping until fluffy. Stir in the reserved onion and any butter left in the dish, 1 cup of the cheese and the teaspoon of parsley. Spoon back into the soufflé dish and sprinkle with the remaining cheese.

Cook on Medium-High for 15 minutes. If you do not have variable power, use either the Medium or Defrost setting and increase the cooking time by 5 to 7 minutes or until heated through. Serve immediately.

NOTE: Reheat leftovers on Medium-High. High power tends to overcook the outside edges.

Wilted Lettuce or Spinach Salad

Serves 4

A simple wilted salad is made even easier by cooking the bacon in the microwave. Both the bacon and the dressing are prepared in the same measuring cup, making cleanup a snap.

6 slices bacon, diced
¼ cup wine vinegar
2 tablespoons water
½ teaspoon salt
¼ teaspoon freshly ground pepper
¼ teaspoon dry mustard
1 head leaf lettuce, torn, or
  1 large bunch spinach, washed
  and stems removed
4 scallions, thinly sliced
1 cup sliced mushrooms
1 hard-cooked egg, grated

Place the bacon in a 4-cup measure, cover with paper towel and cook on High until the bacon is crisp. Remove the bacon with a slotted spoon and drain on paper towel. Add the vinegar, water, salt, pepper and mustard to the drippings and blend well. Cook on High until the mixture boils, about 1 to 2 minutes.

Combine the lettuce, scallions and mushrooms in a large salad bowl. Pour the hot dressing over the lettuce and vegetables and toss lightly. Sprinkle with grated egg and the reserved bacon and serve immediately.

SAUCES

Good cooks know that a sauce can make the simplest dish special, and use them to spruce up almost any kind of food, particularly meat, poultry, vegetables, seafood and eggs — not to mention desserts. Given a few basic techniques and ingredients, sauces are easy to master, even for a beginning cook — and they can be made in almost limitless variety.

Making sauces in a microwave has a number of advantages over conventional methods. You can measure, mix and cook in the same cup or bowl. Cooking time and stirring time are both reduced. Gone is the need to stand over the stove, constantly stirring the sauce and adjusting the heat. Because there is no direct heat to burn the sauce, you never need to scour sticky, burned saucepans.

To insure successful sauces, follow these few basic techniques:

- Always use good-quality unsalted butter for best results.
- Prepare sauces in a container measuring about twice the volume of the ingredients — this will prevent boiling over.
- Stir sauces through several times during cooking, using a wire whisk.
- Avoid opening the oven door too frequently to stir, because it will slow down the cooking.
- To keep made-ahead sauces at the proper temperature, pour them into a warm, dry vacuum bottle or jar.
- Reheat sauces on Medium, timing 1 minute for ½ cup. Add more time as needed. If the sauce seems too thick, add a small amount of hot water before reheating and stir with a

whisk several times both before and after cooking. All the sauces that follow can be reheated, with the exception of Tarragon Sauce (page 72).

• To adapt your own favorite sauces to microwave cooking, just increase the amount of flour or cornstarch slightly, and leave the amount of liquid the same.

Basic White Sauce

Makes about 1 cup

White sauce, or béchamel, is the backbone of many sauces. Use it either plain or in its variations for meat, poultry and vegetable dishes.

3 tablespoons butter, cut into pieces
3 tablespoons flour
¼ teaspoon salt
⅛ teaspoon freshly ground white pepper
1 cup milk, at room temperature

Melt the butter in a 1-quart measure on High, about 30 to 45 seconds. Stir in the flour, salt and pepper. Cook on High for 45 seconds. Slowly whisk in the milk, blending thoroughly. Continue cooking on High for 1 to 2 minutes, just until thickened, stirring once or twice. Serve hot.

Basic white sauce can be covered and refrigerated for up to 2 days. Reheat on Medium until warmed through, adding a small amount of wine or milk if the sauce seems too thick.

Variations:
CHEESE SAUCE: Stir in ½ cup shredded extra-sharp cheddar cheese. Beat until smooth, about 2 minutes. If the cheese has not completely melted, cook on High for 30 seconds and stir again.
MORNAY SAUCE: Add ½ cup shredded Swiss or Parmesan cheese or a combination of both. Sprinkle with ground red pepper and mix until smooth.

(continued)

Variations (continued):

DILL SAUCE: Stir in 1 tablespoon dill weed and 1 tablespoon fresh lemon juice.

CURRY SAUCE: Stir in ½ teaspoon curry powder, or to taste.

VEGETABLE WHITE SAUCE: Use ½ cup milk and ½ cup vegetable poaching or steaming liquid in place of the milk. Stir in 1 teaspoon chopped chives or other chopped or minced fresh herbs.

Tarragon Sauce

Makes about 1½ cups

Serve this aromatic sauce over broiled meat or poultry, poached eggs or a mixture of steamed vegetables.

8 tablespoons butter, melted
½ cup dry white wine or vermouth
1 tablespoon tarragon vinegar
1 tablespoon chopped chives
1 tablespoon chopped fresh tarragon or 1 teaspoon dried, crumbled
½ teaspoon salt
¼ teaspoon freshly ground white pepper
2 drops hot pepper sauce
3 egg yolks

Blend together all the ingredients but the egg yolks in a 2-cup measure. Cook on High for 1 minute. Whisk the egg yolks in a small bowl. Stir a small amount of the butter mixture into the yolks. Stir the yolk mixture into the butter mixture. Cook on Medium for 1 to 2 minutes, stirring after 1 minute. Cook just until smooth and hot.

Fresh Cranberry Sauce

Makes about 2 cups

Once you have prepared your own cranberry sauce, you may never serve canned again! Simply purchase cranberries when they are in season, freeze them in the bag they come in, and enjoy this recipe all year long. Sample the finished product to adjust the sugar to suit your own taste — I prefer mine a little on the tart side.

1 cup water
¾ cup sugar
2 cups fresh or frozen cranberries

Combine the water and sugar in a 2-quart measuring cup or bowl. Cover and bring to a boil on High. Add the berries, cover lightly and continue cooking on High for about 6 minutes, until the berries pop. Stir, and let cool. Turn into a serving bowl and refrigerate until ready to use. Serve with roast turkey, chicken or Cornish game hens.

Barbecue Sauce

Makes about 1½ cups

This barbecue sauce is terrific for chicken, beef roasts and hamburgers. It will keep for several days, covered, in the refrigerator.

⅓ cup chopped onion
2 cloves garlic, finely chopped
1 tablespoon butter
8-ounce can tomato sauce
2 tablespoons dark brown sugar
2 tablespoons fresh lemon juice
1 teaspoon Worcestershire sauce
½ teaspoon salt
¼ teaspoon paprika
¼ teaspoon dry mustard
¼ teaspoon freshly ground pepper
¼ teaspoon crushed red pepper
  (optional)
⅛ teaspoon ground turmeric
  (optional)

Combine the onion, garlic and butter in a 1- or 2-quart measure. Cook on High for 3 minutes. Stir in the remaining ingredients and continue cooking until the sauce is heated through, about 4 minutes.

Custard Sauce

Makes about 2 cups

A custard does not have to be fattening. By making your own you can control the amount of sugar and type of milk. The cornstarch in this recipe insures proper thickening without adding calories.

Scant ¼ cup sugar
1 teaspoon cornstarch
1 teaspoon grated lemon peel
1½ cups low-fat, nonfat or
  skim milk
3 egg yolks
1 teaspoon vanilla

Combine the sugar, cornstarch and lemon peel in a 1-quart measure. Gradually add the milk, stirring constantly until the cornstarch dissolves. Cook, uncovered, on High for about 3 minutes, until the mixture just boils.

Beat the egg yolks in a small bowl. Stir in a small amount of the milk mixture, then whisk into the body of the milk mixture. Cook, uncovered, on High until the custard boils and is thick enough to coat a spoon, about 35 to 60 seconds. Stir in the vanilla. Cover and chill until ready to serve. Serve over fresh fruit or pound cake.

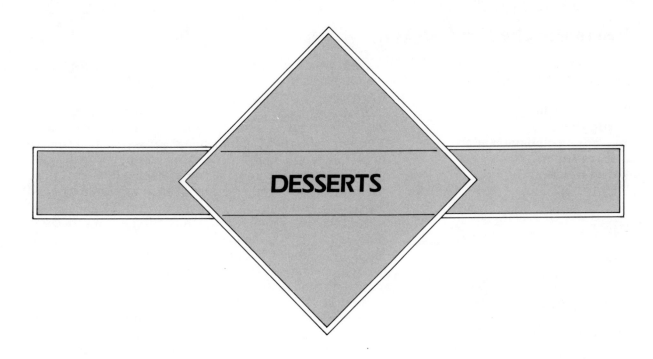

DESSERTS

Many of my favorite desserts are based on fresh fruit. In the spring and summer I make fresh fruit compotes, often with a splash of wine or liqueur, and serve them either on their own or over ice cream. Once you taste a fresh fruit sauce you may never return to overly sweet ice cream sauces.

To insure success in cooking fruit in a microwave, follow these simple techniques:

Always use a deep bowl to allow the juices to boil up without overflowing.

Watch the fruit as it cooks, and when the juices boil up, stir gently and stop cooking.

Always cook fruit on High.

When combining fruits of varying size or firmness, you can, if you wish, maintain the differing textures by cooking each variety separately and combining them after cooking.

Any recipe calling for a double boiler is automatically adaptable to the microwave. Chocolate, for many people the staple of any dessert or candy, doesn't require the usual double-boiler procedure. You simply place it in the microwave to dissolve, then stir it to complete the melting process. No burned chocolate and no scorched pots!

Pears Poached in Red Wine

Serves 4

Poached pears make a special, yet very easy, dessert. Choose a favorite red wine and try to use fresh, firm pears. These may be cooked a day ahead and kept in the refrigerator, tightly covered.

2 cups red wine
¼ cup sugar
3-inch-long cinnamon stick
2 slices lemon
4 firm ripe pears

Combine the wine, sugar, cinnamon stick and lemon slices in a round baking dish or casserole just large enough to hold the pears when arranged in a spoke pattern. Cover and cook on High for 10 minutes, to dissolve the sugar. Peel and core the pears, leaving the stem intact. Cut a thin piece off the bottom of each to allow it to stand upright for serving.

Roll the pears in the syrup and arrange in a spoke pattern, stems facing the center. Cover with wax paper and cook on High for 7 minutes, or until tender. The timing will depend on the ripeness of the pears. Remove from the oven and cool in the syrup, occasionally spooning it over the pears.

To serve, stand each pear in an attractive bowl and serve with the red wine syrup or raspberry sauce. Or cut the pears in half and serve with a scoop of vanilla ice cream in each center.

Fresh Fruit Compote

Serves 4 to 6

Briefly cooking fresh fruit for a compote heightens the already rich flavors, making them intense and even more appealing.

2 peaches, quartered and pitted
4 apricots, halved and pitted
4 plums, halved and pitted
10 cherries, halved and pitted
1 small bunch seedless grapes

Combine the fruits in a 3-quart bowl. Cook, uncovered, on High for about 7 to 10 minutes, just until the juices boil. Let stand 1 minute, then stir gently. Allow to cool slightly in the juices. Serve warm, at room temperature or chilled.

Applesauce

Serves 1

Applesauce makes a wholesome low-calorie dessert or snack that is both easy to prepare and delicious, especially when made with strawberries. To make additional servings, increase the cooking time by 2 minutes per apple.

1 tart cooking apple, peeled
   (if desired), cored and sliced
¼ teaspoon cinnamon
6 strawberries (optional)

Arrange the apple slices in a 2-cup baking dish and sprinkle with the cinnamon. Cover and cook on High for 3 minutes. Transfer to a food processor, add the strawberries and blend to the desired consistency.

Cream Cheese Pie with Sour Cream Topping

Serves 8

The technique for making this cheese pie, or cheesecake, is a little different from most, and the result is superbly dense and rich.

2 8-ounce packages cream cheese,
   at room temperature
2 eggs
½ cup sugar
1 tablespoon grated lemon peel
1½ teaspoons vanilla
⅛ teaspoon salt
2 cups sour cream
9-inch graham cracker crust
¼ cup sugar

Combine the cream cheese and eggs in a small bowl and beat until fluffy. Add the sugar, lemon peel, vanilla and salt and blend well. Add 1 cup of the sour cream and mix thoroughly. Cook on High for 8 minutes, stopping every 2 minutes to stir with a whisk. Pour into the crust and let cool.

Combine the remaining sour cream and sugar and blend well. Spread evenly over the pie. Chill thoroughly before serving.

Pie Shell

Pie shells should always be precooked before filling. Brushing the pastry with egg yolk before cooking gives it an attractive golden color. Use this pie shell for pies or quiches.

1 **cup flour**
½ **teaspoon salt**
⅓ **cup solid vegetable shortening**
3 **tablespoons cold water**
1 **egg yolk, slightly beaten**

Mix together the flour and salt and cut in the shortening until it resembles coarse meal. Add the water, and mix just until it forms a soft workable ball.

Refrigerate for about 20 minutes. Shape the dough into a flat circle on a floured surface. Roll out the circle to fit a 9-inch pie plate or quiche dish. Fold into quarters and gently transfer to the pie plate. Unfold the crust without stretching it. Build up and flute the edge. Brush the whole surface with the slightly beaten egg yolk and prick with a fork.

Cook on High 6 to 7 minutes until the shell is crisp and brown spots appear.

NOTE: Frozen pie shells can be transferred easily from the metal pie tin to a glass or ceramic pie plate or quiche dish. Allow the pastry to defrost completely in the new plate and then flute the edge attractively. Brush with egg yolk, as above, and prick well to prevent puffing. Cook as directed.

Pecan Pie

This deliciously rich pie will last about as long as it takes to cook it, so be prepared to make it often. A scoop of ice cream or a dollop of whipped cream make it extra-special.

4 **tablespoons unsalted butter**
1½ **cups pecan halves**
1 **cup sugar**
½ **cup light or dark corn syrup**
3 **eggs, lightly beaten**
1 **teaspoon vanilla**
9-inch pie shell, baked (see above)

Melt the butter in a 2-quart measure on High. Add the nuts, sugar, corn syrup, eggs and vanilla and blend well. Pour into the baked pie shell. Cook on Medium-High until the center is set, about 12 minutes. Serve at room temperature or chilled.

Grasshopper Pie

Grasshopper pie is a good party dessert, for it is both festive and easy to prepare in advance. This recipe saves the step of whipping egg whites and sugar by using marshmallows instead.

1½ cups chocolate wafer crumbs
¼ cup melted butter
4 cups miniature marshmallows
½ cup milk
¼ cup white crème de cacao
¼ cup green crème de menthe
2 cups whipped cream
1 ounce semi-sweet chocolate

Mix together the cookie crumbs and butter and press into a 9-inch pie plate. Cook on High for about 45 seconds, until set. Cool slightly and refrigerate.

Combine the marshmallows and milk in a 2-quart bowl. Cook on High until the marshmallows begin to melt, about 2 to 2½ minutes. Stir until completely melted. Cool slightly, blend in the liqueurs and cool completely.

Fold in 1½ cups of the whipped cream. Spoon the mixture into the prepared crust. Garnish with the remaining whipped cream. Grate as much of the chocolate as desired over the pie, or sprinkle with chocolate curls made with a vegetable peeler. Refrigerate until firm. Serve chilled.

Brownies

Double-chocolate brownies are the dream of many chocolate lovers. These are infinitely satisfying — to make and to eat.

Remember: Chocolate does not dissolve completely until it is stirred, so you run the risk of overcooking it if you leave it in the oven too long. Remove it from the microwave as soon as it turns shiny, then stir until it is completely melted.

2 ounces unsweetened baking chocolate
8 tablespoons unsalted butter
2 eggs
¾ cup sugar
½ cup flour
1 tablespoon vanilla
1 teaspoon baking powder
¼ teaspoon salt
1 cup coarsely chopped walnuts
1 cup chocolate chips

Combine the chocolate and butter in a measuring cup and cook on High until the butter is melted, about 1½ minutes. Stir to blend.

Beat the eggs lightly in a large bowl. Add the chocolate mixture, sugar, flour, vanilla, baking powder and salt and blend thoroughly. Stir in the nuts and chocolate chips. Turn into a greased 9-inch pie plate or quiche dish and cook on High for 6 minutes. (Turn, if it appears to be cooking unevenly.) The mixture will still be moist, but will firm up as it cools.

Cool completely before cutting into squares.

Chocolate Cocoa Cake with
Almond Custard Filling

Serves 10 to 12

If you are a chocolate and almond fan, this dessert is well worth the preparation time, for the cake is moist and the filling rich. You will need a round, deep cake pan designed for microwave ovens. Handle the delicate cake gently, because it crumbles easily.

2 cups sugar
1¾ cups flour
¾ cup unsweetened cocoa powder
2 teaspoons baking soda
1 teaspoon baking powder
1 teaspoon salt
2 eggs, at room temperature
¾ cup strong coffee
1 teaspoon instant coffee crystals
¾ cup buttermilk
½ cup vegetable oil
1 teaspoon vanilla

ALMOND CUSTARD FILLING:
1 cup milk
2 eggs, at room temperature
2 egg yolks
1 cup sugar
¼ cup flour
3 tablespoons unsalted butter
2 teaspoons vanilla
½ teaspoon almond liqueur
(Amaretto)
½ cup toasted almonds, finely
chopped

FROSTING:
12 tablespoons (6 ounces) unsalted
butter
1¼ cups cocoa powder
3½ cups confectioners' sugar
½ cup milk
2 teaspoons vanilla

To make the cake, blend together the sugar, flour, cocoa, baking soda, baking powder and salt. Beat together the eggs, coffee, instant coffee, buttermilk, oil and vanilla. Add to the dry ingredients and blend well.

Grease the sides of an 8-inch round microwave cake pan. Line the bottom with parchment. Pour in half the batter. Cook on High for 6 to 6½ minutes, turning several times if the cake begins cooking unevenly. Cool in the pan on a rack for 10 minutes, then turn the cake out onto the rack and let it cool completely. Wash and dry the pan, then grease and line it as before and cook the remaining half of the batter. When both layers have completely cooled, cut each cake in half horizontally, making 4 layers.

To make the filling, start by scalding the milk in a 4-cup glass measure on High for 2 minutes. Blend together the eggs, egg yolks, sugar, flour and scalded milk. Cook the mixture on High for 2 minutes. Continue cooking, stirring every 30 seconds until the mixture is thick, about 2 minutes. Stir in the butter, vanilla, almond liqueur and toasted almonds. Beat for about 1 minute, until smooth.

To make the frosting, put the butter in a 2-quart bowl and melt 45 seconds on High. Blend in the cocoa and cook on High an additional 30 seconds. Set aside to cool. Add the sugar and milk, alternately, and beat to a smooth spreading consistency. Stir in the vanilla.

To assemble the cake, set 1 layer on a serving platter. Spread with one-third of the filling. Add the second layer and cover with another third of the filling. Add the third layer and spread with the remaining filling. Add the fourth layer and cover the top and sides of the cake with the frosting. Serve at room temperature or chilled.

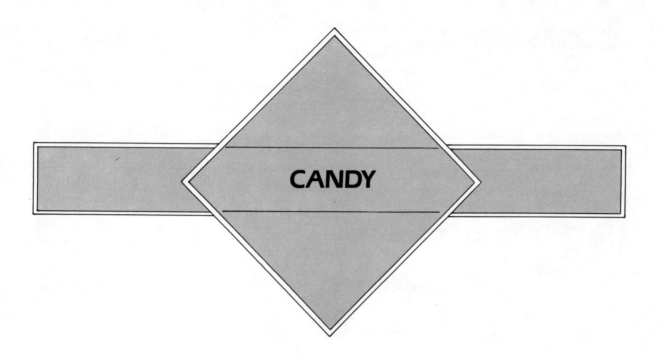

CANDY

The microwave oven has taken the mystery out of candy-making. In no time, the savvy microwave cook can turn out an unlimited supply of wonderful candy that will keep neighborhood trick-or-treaters, family and friends happy all through a holiday season.

Perhaps the greatest advantage of the microwave in making candy is the absence of direct heat to scorch and overcook. Because the heat is more uniform and the microwave energy keeps the ingredients in constant motion, constant stirring is less important than in conventional candy-making.

Monitoring the temperature is essential in making candy. Microwave candy thermometers can be used during cooking. Standard candy termometers cannot be used in the microwave, but can, of course, be used to test the temperature after cooking. Sugars get extremely hot, so always use a bowl that can tolerate high temperatures, and preferably one with a handle. Always keep pot holders handy.

Milk Chocolate Fudge

Makes about 1 pound

The creamy texture and great flavor combine to make this a favorite recipe of my students. Chopped maraschino cherries give additional flavor and color. Warning: Do not try this recipe if you are dieting — it is so simple to make, it might be a temptation to keep the ingredients on hand!

12 ounces milk chocolate chips
¼ cup evaporated milk
⅛ teaspoon salt
½ teaspoon vanilla
10 maraschino cherries,
**   drained and chopped**
¾ cup coarsely chopped walnuts

Lightly butter an 8-inch-square pan. Combine the chocolate chips, milk and salt in a 1-quart glass measure. Cook on High until the chocolate chips turn shiny, about 2-2½ minutes. Add the vanilla and stir until smooth. Blend in the chopped cherries and walnuts. Pour the fudge into the prepared pan and let cool until firm. Cut into ½- or 1-inch squares and serve.

Chocolate-Coffee Truffles

Makes about 4 dozen

These rich chocolate candies can compete with the most expensive commercial truffles, and they make a lovely gift to bring to a chocolate-loving friend. Truffles freeze well if arranged on sheets of wax paper; once frozen, they can be transferred to a covered freezer container. Always use a good-quality chocolate — it really does make all the difference!

12 ounces semi-sweet chocolate,
**   broken into pieces**
4 egg yolks
½ cup coffee liqueur (Kahlua)
⅔ cup unsalted butter, softened
Unsweetened cocoa, ground
**   almonds, or confectioners' sugar**

Melt the chocolate in a 1-quart measure on High for 2 minutes. Stir until smooth. Let cool almost to room temperature. Beat in the egg yolks, one at a time. Blend in the liqueur. Cook on High for 30 seconds. Add the softened butter a tablespoon at a time, beating well after each addition. Continue beating until the mixture is light and fluffy, about 4 or 5 minutes. Cover with plastic wrap and chill in the refrigerator for 2 to 3 hours.

Roll the chocolate into ¾-inch balls, and coat with cocoa, almonds or confectioners' sugar.

Almond Bark

White chocolate is a particular favorite of many people who love candy. Here it is teamed with almond in a delicious and very simple confection. White chocolate is sold in bulk in specialty food stores.

1 cup blanched whole almonds
1 teaspoon butter
1 pound white chocolate,
  broken into pieces

Combine the almonds and butter in a 9-inch pie plate and cook on High, stirring once or twice, until the almonds are toasted, about 4 or 5 minutes.

Line a baking sheet with wax paper and set aside. Cook the chocolate in a 2-quart bowl on High just until softened, about 1½ to 2 minutes. Do not overcook or the chocolate will become grainy. Stir in the almonds and blend well. Spread the mixture onto the lined baking sheet. Refrigerate until set and break into pieces to serve.

Peanut Brittle

This is the best peanut brittle I have ever tasted. After you have tried it, you will probably never buy commercial peanut brittle again! For a variation, try making it with pecans, walnuts, or a can of assorted nuts.

1 cup sugar
½ cup light or dark corn syrup
1¾-2 cups dry roasted unsalted
  peanuts
1 teaspoon unsalted butter
1 teaspoon baking soda

Generously grease a baking sheet. Combine the sugar and corn syrup in a 2-quart bowl and cook on High for 4 minutes. Stir in the peanuts, using a wooden spoon. Continue cooking on High for 3 minutes. Stir in the butter and vanilla and cook until a candy thermometer registers 300 degrees or a small amount of the mixture separates into hard and brittle threads when dropped into ice water, about 2 to 2½ minutes. Blend in the baking soda and stir until the mixture is light and foamy.

Pour onto the prepared baking sheet and spread quickly to the edges, using the back of a wooden spoon. Grease your hands, and as the candy cools, stretch it into a thin sheet with your palms. Let it cool completely, then break into pieces. Store in an airtight container in a cool place.

Lollipops

Lollipops are great fun to make with children, who find few things as exciting as making their own candies for birthday or Halloween parties. An adult should handle the hot sugar syrup, but children can do the creative work of forming and decorating the lollipops.

10 lollipop sticks
¾ cup sugar
½ cup light corn syrup
4 tablespoons unsalted butter
1 teaspoon flavoring or extract
    (peppermint, orange, vanilla,
    cinnamon, etc.)
Food coloring
Cinnamon candies or other
    miniature candies for decoration

Arrange the sticks on parchment paper, spacing them at least 4 inches apart.

Combine the sugar, corn syrup and butter in a 2-quart heat-resistant bowl. Cook on High for 2 minutes. Stir in the flavoring and food coloring. Continue cooking on High for 5 to 7 minutes, until a candy thermometer registers 270 degrees, or until a small amount of the mixture separates into threads that are hard but not brittle when dropped into very cold water. Drop the syrup by tablespoons over one end of each stick. Press candies gently into place. Let cool completely. Wrap each in plastic and store in an airtight container.